"At a time when the world is crying for better leaders, Ken Jennings and Mike McCormick have produced a winner. *House on Fire* is powerful storytelling, but so much more! Patterned after what Jesus both taught and modeled about servant leadership, this book skillfully lays out the nuts and bolts to show readers 'how' to improve their Serving Leadership."

—**Chaplain (Colonel) Scott McChrystal**, USA (Retired). Military Representative, Assemblies of God Chaplaincy Ministries

"*House on Fire* by my friend Ken Jennings and Mike McCormick is a tale of leadership and life shaping decisions, set in a gripping story of powerful relationships and choices. Leaders looking to shape and sharpen their leadership will find this book to be a ready and helpful guide to everyday effectiveness. The story is compelling, and the content is engaging. Read this book now!"

—**John Jackson**, President, William Jessup University

"Is Servant Leadership good in for-profit or non-profit organizations? In both settings, the answer is an unequivocal yes and always. *House on Fire* illustrates the power of serving in Christian organizations — by showing us how deep relationships paired with courageous goals, accountability, and support unlock amazing outcomes. Don't miss these life lessons for your work and the community you serve!"

— **Cheryl Bachelder**, Author, *Dare to Serve: How to Drive Superior Results by Serving Others*. Former CEO of Popeyes Louisiana Kitchen, Inc.

"*House on Fire* is a rare combination of great and proven content on leadership and a page-turning story all told against the backdrop of the college campus. It is an entertaining and edifying read for anyone, but will have special significance for those involved in ministry to college students and other young adults. Read, learn, enjoy and share!"

"Fascinating. I read this book in one sitting. The story line is captivating, and the principles are compelling. A must read for anyone committed to serving and leading a movement of multiplication. Well done."

"Ken, Mike, and their team have been instrumental in developing our MCYM leaders and aligning our ministry strategy into the future. *House on Fire* is a compelling story that brings leadership to life in the real world of ministry. It is a much-needed practical book that I wish I would have had earlier in my ministry career. Now that it's here, I recommend it to every ministry leader."

"The hallmark of Applied Servant Leadership involves an emphasis on the needs of others, enabling them to learn, grow and excel. It has been successfully applied in business settings, academics, healthcare, and athletics to augment the values an organization holds true. In this faith-based allegory, Serving Leadership facilitates the central character to transcend the human condition and understand the nature of faith lost and found."

—**Colleen Koch**, MD, MS, MBA Professor and Chair,
Department of Anesthesiology and Critical Care Medicine,
Johns Hopkins Medicine

"In *House on Fire*, Ken Jennings and Mike McCormick combine rich use of a metaphor, an engaging narrative style, creative graphics, and a generous offering of back-of-the-book resources in presenting five key and guiding principles for Applied Servant Leadership."

—**Gary Moon**, Executive Director of the Martin Institute for
Christianity and Culture and the Dallas Willard Center for
Christian Spiritual Formation at Westmont College

"*House on Fire* uses a great storytelling approach to illustrate and show application for very important leadership principles that all Serving Leaders should pay attention to. Thanks Ken and Mike for doing the work to make these principles come alive."

—**Dr. Sandra Gray**, Former President, Asbury University

"Ken Jennings and Mike McCormick have written a masterful book. It not only has an engaging story line, but when you finish the book you will have received the equivalent of an advanced degree in 'Serving Leadership' based on Christ like leadership principles. I highly recommend this book for all who are in or aspire to leadership positions."

—**Kerry Alberti**, Chairman, Board of Directors of Military Community Youth Ministries; Trustee Emeritus and retired Chief Financial Officer of Young Life

"*House on Fire* is thought-provoking, practical, and insightful. I believe the principles presented in this easy-to-read narrative will capture the hearts and imagination of the next generation of leaders in the Church."

—**Linnette Bachman**, Campus Minister, The Navigators

Nanette,

Thank you for doing your
part to live, love, & lead
like Jesus!

Matt 5:14-16

House on Fire! Mike McConal

Keith Jmys

HOUSE
ON
FIRE!

A STORY OF
LOSS, LOVE & SERVANT LEADERSHIP

KEN JENNINGS
Best-selling co-author of *The Serving Leader*

MIKE MCCORMICK

NASHVILLE

NEW YORK • LONDON • MELBOURNE • VANCOUVER

House on Fire!

A Story of Loss, Love & Servant Leadership

Published in New York, New York, by Morgan James Publishing. Morgan James is a trademark of Morgan James, LLC. www.MorganJamesPublishing.com

All characters in *House on Fire* are fictional. All combat scenes were written by D.L. Jennings and were reviewed and approved by the Department of Defense.

Unless otherwise noted, Scripture quotations taken from The Holy Bible, New International Version® NIV® Copyright © 1973, 1978, 1984, 2011 by Biblica, Inc.™ Used by permission. All rights reserved worldwide.

ISBN 9781642794878 paperback
ISBN 9781642794885 eBook
ISBN 9781642794892 audio
Library of Congress Control Number: 2019901527

Cover Design by:
Christopher Kirk
www.GFSstudio.com

Interior Design by:
Chris Treccani
www.3dogcreative.net

Morgan James is a proud partner of Habitat for Humanity Peninsula and Greater Williamsburg. Partners in building since 2006.

Get involved today! Visit
MorganJamesPublishing.com/giving-back

"Daughter, son, step into the light."
-D.L. JENNINGS,
Award Winning Novelist, *Gift of the Shaper*

"The aim of God in history is the creation of an all-inclusive community of loving persons, with Himself included in that community as its prime sustainer and most glorious inhabitant."
-DALLAS WILLARD

CONTENTS

FOREWORD

Service, sacrifice, and love are perhaps not the words you would expect to be used to describe a singular approach to living and leading others, but they belong together. Ken Jennings and Mike McCormick elegantly stitch these words to each other in their new book, *House on Fire*.

My leadership research and life experience have taught me that servant leadership is the best way to lead—because leaders who serve first and lead second achieve both great relationships and great results. Servant leadership has become a movement not only in this country but also around the world. *House on Fire* will show you practical servant leader actions you can take to become a better leader as well as the heart reasons behind those actions.

Ken and Mike have written a book you won't be able to put down. It's an engaging and exciting story—a fast-paced adventure about a young woman on a quest. Like every quest, this journey contains a worthwhile prize, unpredictable danger, and the opportunity to learn important truths. I think you'll enjoy each of these elements—and maybe encounter some surprises along the way.

As you read *House on Fire,* you'll see a practical servant leadership model woven throughout the book. And as you finish, you'll find how to get advice to lead differently at work and in the community. Who knew you could enjoy a book and learn so much at the same time!

I believe *House on Fire* will light a flame inside you to serve, lead, and commit to pursuing the Ultimate Servant Leader in the company of others. This is a book you'll want to share with your friends as you learn together and grow in community. At the end of the story, the call to action by Rev. Lee Scott will help you think about how you can connect to the servant leadership movement in which Ken, Mike, and I all play a part.

Enjoy the story. Join the movement!

—**Ken Blanchard**, co-author of *The New One Minute Manager*®
and *Servant Leadership in Action*

IN THE DARK

The resilient, battle-tested Byron Washington—who a few years later would save me—arrived in my city needing help. The stump that had once been his right leg was causing him serious pain and badly needed more repair. Nothing hurt just now, though, as the experienced VA anesthesiologist eased him into blackness. A determined surgical team went right to work. Outside the surgical suite, a tight group of military men discussed their friend.

The group was headed by a bearded 'operator,' a narrow special ops designation. His *nom de guerre* was 'Dog.' He knew Byron well, and he knew what he wanted for his currently unconscious friend.

"He will need a new mission and a new team. My sister is in school here and she raves about the ministry on campus," he told the group. "Byron was the best downrange medic we ever had, but he was just as good as a chaplain, unofficially of course. When he wakes up, my sister and some of the ministry staff are going to come over. I think if we position how much this ministry needs a leader like Byron, he just might recruit himself. We can help, right fellas?"

"Right, Dog!" they replied in unison. The usually invisible team was drawing stares in the waiting area.

Eventually, a tired surgeon stepped out of the suite. He looked worried, and his gown was spattered with blood. He was ex-Army and he was blunt.

"Sorry, I should have changed. We had problems. Your buddy Byron is a vascular mess. We had to get creative. I wish I could do more, but he's still going to have pain and function challenges."

"Challenges? Oh, he's had plenty of those," Dog said. "He's not going to have us this time, though ..."

* * *

Two years later, I was a reporter living in a city on fire. Arsons were becoming frequent and scary. No one had any leads. I'm Sophie Alsas. I wanted to be on the story, but I wasn't allowed; I was still earning my way up.

This particular morning, I had showered and made breakfast when Ben, my editor, called. He never called me at home.

"Sophie," Ben said over the phone, "I've got a story I want to talk about with you in my office. Thirty minutes?" I doubted he had something real, but instead was simply feeling sorry for me. I quickly grabbed a blue blazer and headed to the office downtown.

A dark, almost black sky framed the mix of historic and modern architecture that lined the narrow urban streets as my Jeep took me through the heart of Pittsburgh. There was a fast-moving storm coming in. The Appalachians around the city acted as a funnel, increasing the intensity of the storm as it moved south from the Great Lakes. It soon would be a metaphor for my life, though I didn't know it yet.

Pittsburgh is a patchwork of ethnic neighborhoods and tech start-ups. Polish Hill, Little Italy, Greek and Russian Orthodox churches stood cheek-to-cheek with Google, robotics companies, and college campuses. Up and down the Appalachian hills I went, the dramatic downtown view jumping out at me as my bright yellow Jeep emerged from the Hill District. There was my black steel office tower, looming above the city's landmark three rivers. Silver, yellow, and red steel bridges surround the city like colored gems on river necklaces.

At my office skyscraper, I took the external clear glass elevator. Rising above the landscape, I could see the mix of clear and dark muddy water at the turbulent confluence of the two merging rivers, the Monongahela and the Allegheny, fusing at the city's Point State Park to form a third river—the Ohio. I often wandered down to the point to witness the churning power of the confluence.

Three young guys in expensive European suits—no ties— got on the elevator at a middle financial services floor, staring directly at me as they entered. I shot a "back off" look in their direction and jammed the button for the next floor, brusquely pushing past them as soon as the door opened. I still had five floors to go, but I preferred to take the stairs the rest of the way up to avoid their stares.

I focused on my meeting ahead as I climbed. *Deep breaths Sophie, you're going to see Ben-the-Legend.* Ben has been a force in the newspaper world since he entered it. His tough but caring style helped him succeed at all levels. He went to college at Carnegie Mellon University and rose to editor of the school newspaper by his sophomore year. After college he worked for the *New York Times,* first as an investigative journalist, then as associate editor. Eventually, he was offered the job of editor in chief back here at the *Pittsburgh Herald.* He was tough but somehow always on my side. And even though he scared me, I loved to be around him.

As I walked across the newsroom floor, I managed to trip slightly right in front of Ben's glass office door. My coffee bean earrings jingled as I caught myself and looked around to see who noticed my fall. Ben laughed, waving me in with a sheaf of papers and a smile, setting me further on edge. The Legend was laughing at me.

"Get in here! I've got a story for you, Sophie." Ben was short, bald, and looked like he had just walked off the set of an old-time newspaper movie. He fanned out the pile of papers on the desk between us. I could see a stack of marked-up articles, presumably intended for me.

"What have you got? I hope it's just as exciting as your last 'learn the local court system' idea," I said. I could still recount the playbill of local attorneys I could not make up in fiction; colorful and skillful in dealing via shorthand legal maneuvers with court officials. I had learned much, truth be told. I knew Ben wanted me to succeed, with his creative assignments and constant coaching. He made all of us around him better at what we were doing. He was a leader.

Ben's mother was Puerto Rican, so he spoke Spanish fluently. To keep my rapport with The Legend, I always spoke a little Spanish with him. I liked to give him faux grief while others were too intimidated.

More background: Ben and my mother, Sara Alsas, have been friends for a long time. They were classmates together in Pittsburgh, at Schenley High School, and reconnected years later at church when Mom relocated us to Pittsburgh. Ben helped get Mom a job teaching writing at Pitt and hired me. He wanted me to do features about the community and people. I took the job but wanted to get into more exciting assignments. The *Pittsburgh Herald* is known as one of the best high purpose news organizations in the country and enjoys a positive national reputation, even as news organizations everywhere are under pressure. Ben was a great leader in a challenging business and I was lucky to work for him. Mom was delighted to have me close by. Secretly-not-so-secretly, I know Mom and Ben conspired to plan my life. Both are 'helicopters.'

"Sophie, I want you to do an investigative piece on a campus ministry called 'The House,'" Ben was telling me. "It's a Christian ministry with a national reputation for positive impacts and using Servant Leadership to do their work. Our readers need something good to offset the never-ending negative news sludge."

"*La plena,* really? That's not investigation, Ben."

Ben countered, "The House is a solid story. They do plenty of good things on campus and in the community."

"You got this 'story' from Mom, no?"

"Sophie," he raised his finger, "Don't start. There's another reason this is in your wheelhouse, it's Christian. There *is* a story in here, trust me. I need an insider—someone who can speak the language."

Ben knew I could do that.

I had infiltration ability because I was an MK, a missionary kid, which is a church gold star. My dad was a church planter and a missionary who had died 'heroically,' so I could talk the talk. But for me, his death destroyed my home—and eventually my desire to stay connected to Christian community. I only write about community now. I'd written dozens of community-centric stories for Ben. Truth be told, I liked telling the stories of real people and families. Maybe I was trying to recreate what I lost. Anyway, I knew—and was known—in a dozen tight-knit communities around Pittsburgh.

Mom made sure I grew up in a storytelling home. Even back then, I wrote little stories with her help. She was a gifted writer and teacher of writing, and I hoped to take after her. But I was keenly aware that I was a work in progress.

Ben was getting impatient, or at least pretending to be. "Get going on this. Why are you still here?" He tap, tap, tapped a stubby pencil on his desk to model his finite patience.

I pulled at my suede kitten heels. *Time to be a professional, Sophie.*

"Sí. You hired me to write, Ben," I fake smiled.

"Good, you're perfect for this. I don't want to be proven wrong."

My smile tightened further, "I'll make you happy." I hesitated, then added, "Ben can you maybe give me a little more to go on besides, 'go investigate The House?'"

"Yeah, okay, I'll help you get started." He grabbed a blank sheet of paper and wrote:

See Differently – Serve Differently

"Here you go. This is a basis of The House's Applied Servant Leadership model and good work track record. Why aren't you taking notes?"

"I am," I hastily replied and took out my notebook. I had been thrown off by these strange words and the unexpected Christian talk. What was with my no-nonsense editor?

"Go investigate how The House puts this model to work with students and the community around them. You will find that the alumni of The House are effective everywhere they serve. They wind up in plenty of high consequence and interesting places. That's the story. I'm expecting a thorough piece so I'm keeping the rest of your schedule light. 'See Differently and Serve Differently' are The House's leadership principles. Start your story there."

This was apparently a big deal to Ben. I sat there looking at the four words he'd written. "Well, I'm not going to write the piece for you!" He pushed the single sheet of paper across to me.

"That's all I get? A T-shirt level slogan?"

"That's all I got to start with myself. The team at The House will add more and help you understand." What did he mean by 'that's all I got to start with myself?' Mysterious. I didn't go there, but I did ask again:

"Ben, did you get this idea from Mom?"

"We did discuss it, yes, but it's mostly the times. Positive stories are still important to our readers. But hey, your mom would actually be a great place to start."

"Noted. Anything else you can give me to get started?"

"Yep. The House is affiliated with a second, very different house out in the community. I'll let you find out about it."

I should have seen something coming right there.

"I just sent you Luke Jarrell's email and phone number. He's the ministry leader at The House. But like I said, start with this," he said, glaring and pointing to the paper. "Your T-shirt slogan."

I stared at it, not touching it. Ben watched me, with a grouchy, slow-emerging smile. "Take it and get to work."

I took the paper and retreated to my cubicle in the newsroom. I got myself mentally ready to re-enter a Christian world. I didn't want to. My dad died in that world, a continent away.

For a while after my dad died on the mission field, I believed Jesus would miraculously bring him back if I prayed hard enough. I tried hard to believe, maybe thinking that would force His hand? But it did not.

Eventually, I stopped believing in much at all.

FIRST SOURCE

I was absorbing my surprising assignment when my cell phone brought me back to reality. "*Hola* Mom, you must have read my mind." I was totally suspicious. "I was going to call you about my new story."

My mother's cheerful, alluring voice came lilting over the phone. "No, I was just thinking about you. Could you stop over on your way home from downtown?" Mom must have been tipped off that I had just met with Ben.

Conspiracy!

"I'd love to, Mom. I'm still training for the Pittsburgh Sprint Triathlon, so I'd like to get a workout in. I'm struggling with the swim and need the practice. The way my swimming is now I'm nowhere near ready for a triathlon."

"Whenever works for you, dear. Come when you can. *Te quiero.*"

There was some strange urgency in Mom's voice, so I promised I to come straight from the pool 'as long as I didn't drown.'

I struggled in the pool. Running on land is my happy place. Thrashing in the water is difficult and exhausting. I headed to my mother's place in the Hill District, listening to classical music. In her driveway, I switched to Outlaw Country, my U.S. cultural project. I sat for a few minutes trying to get the lyrics. I like the music, but the words still baffle me. I could see my mother through the large arched living room window, the Christmas lights from last year still outlining the frame.

My mom was my best friend, so I'm sure my backsliding from my faith hurt her deeply. I was glad Dad wasn't around to see it.

My mother, Sara Edith Alsas, was a missionary daughter herself. She was born on the mission field in Mali and returned to the states on a regular basis with my grandparents to the Lancaster area of eastern Pennsylvania. Later, they moved their home base to Pittsburgh to be near the mission headquarters and medical care for my grandfather. His declining health eventually forced my grandparents off the mission field for good in the '90s. My grandfather, still passionate for 'The Kingdom,' became a church planter in the States. He never stopped. I was one of his current projects. He sent me frequent letters and books that I read out of respect, but I ignored the Christian advice.

Mom went off to college at Wheaton near Chicago where she met Dad in Glee Club. Music filled our home as I grew up. Unfortunately, I did not inherit their talent.

Through the window I could see Mom organizing her standing desk, her smooth hair tied up at the nape of her neck. People would always say I looked just like her, tall and lean. The main difference between us was our hair. Mine was various shades of copper while Mom's was a chestnut brown, now streaked with grey.

Over the years she gained some wrinkles, but she earned them with her joyful smiles. She hugged me often whenever I visited her. Her hugs were threads connecting me back to when I felt loved and at home.

I'd sat outside her house many times, watching her before going in, imagining I could see Dad with her. I tried to remember every detail of what he looked like, how he walked, and his habit of spinning us both around at unexpected times. He wanted us to 'practice our dancing' for heaven. I was a fairytale princess at a ball. But after his death, I stopped dancing.

I stayed watching her a moment longer before getting out of my Jeep and walking to the slightly ajar front door. She never locked her door because she trusted people and I suppose, God. It had worked so far.

"Mom?" I said as I pushed in.

"Sophie, *mi amor!*" she exclaimed, giving me a tender mom hug. "You're so… fit."

"Well, I'm trying." I made a muscle and she giggled.

"*En serio.* You said you have some work things you wanted to ask me about? *¿Qué fue?*" Mom prompted. I knew that she knew about the story.

"I'm on something that could be interesting. You may have heard about it from Ben?" I gave her a knowing look. She just smiled and nodded for me to continue. "I'm looking into a campus ministry house around here and I'm going to meet Luke Jarrell, the head of the ministry, tomorrow."

Mom was ready. "I know Luke, his team and the House well. It's a terrific discipleship and leadership house. Luke has a great group of staff you *have* to get to know. They're so *amiguero!* They go into the heart of seeing and leading differently."

Yep, Mom was going to be my first source. *God, you're clever.* I still talked to Him even though we were estranged. I might as well go with the plan. "I'd love your help, Mom. Can you tell me what you know about this place, the House?" I sat down and pulled out my reporter's notebook.

"Is this to be an interview?" Mom said playfully, sitting down and pulling a bright South American shawl over her shoulders. I remember when she got it from a woman in our *barrio*.

"*Sí*, I guess so. Tell me what you know."

I watched her collect her thoughts. She smiled shyly at me and began.

"I adore the House. I love the ministry, the leadership, and the work they do so I'm a biased source, dear. I walk by the House every day on my way to teach my 9 a.m. freshman writing class. The House is a very well-known and highly effective ministry. Luke's a terrific leader. He and the staff there are known for developing disciples who continue to grow in Christ and have what it takes to serve, lead, and make a difference in their jobs, churches, and community when they leave campus. They use and teach an applied form of Servant Leadership to do their work."

I recognized my story leads and wrote them down.

- Known for alumni who serve, lead, and make a difference

- Applied Servant Leadership – What is it?

"Okay, go on."

"Students from all over the country and the world as well as young adults from the community are involved at the House. They all come with wildly different faith foundations. This is a time when many make up their own minds about Christ rather than still simply borrowing their parents' faith."

My cheeks grew hot.

Mom moved her hands about as she talked, reminding me of the expressive way Alba, my "second *madre"* in Ecuador, spoke. "The House welcomes all of them. They're good at including everyone who comes and creating a real community for people to join. The aim of The House is to create disciples who 'do all that Jesus said and did himself.' As I said, they also prepare students to lead well wherever they go. That Servant Leadership focus is a distinction."

"*¿La plena* Mom?"

"Really, I've seen it up close. Seek the truth and you will find it, dear."

We both laughed at her intentionally over-the-top words. I was her straying prodigal daughter, and she never stopped longing for me to come home. I anticipated what was coming next.

"While you're investigating, pay attention to what your own heart says about what you are learning."

"Are you trying to get me 'back' again, Mom?"

She didn't flinch. "That would be the answer to what I pray every day, *mi amor.* But no, I'm just asking you to experience the story. If it leads you back to the faith of your childhood, you'll see me rejoice."

"Well don't get your hopes up. I'm not finished falling yet—falling from grace, that is."

"You don't fall from grace, you fall *to* grace. That was something your dad said."

"Okay, Mom, I probably should get going."

She hesitated. "Wait, about your dad, I've got something for you." A look of anxiety settled on her face, her hands trembling.

"*¿Qué más*, Mom?"

SOLO

Mom got up, clutched her bright, multi-colored alpaca shawl around her like a protective cape, and walked unsteadily into the other room. She came back with the past.

"This is from your dad's plane," she said. I recognized his battered metal flight map case. "I could never bring myself to open it until just this week. I'd put it away after it was recovered all those years ago."

Seeing the case, I held my breath. I'd imagined the struggle in the air many times. A wire shorted somewhere and an electrical fire sparked in flight. This is an extreme emergency. Dad was solo in the high mountains fighting a growing fire—an aviator's greatest fear. The only option is to somehow extinguish the fire and get on the ground.

In the mountains, he would not have had an emergency landing field. He would have grabbed the fire extinguisher and tried to fight the flames. Search crews found the extinguisher emptied. He fought to the end.

I know he did not panic; he never panicked. I know he was brave; he was always brave. At the end, he would have prayed out loud for me and Mom with his last breaths. How I wished I could tell him I loved him just one more time. But we had argued the previous night. I told him I hated him and I never wanted to fly with him again. The next morning, he did not wake me up to go with him. I never lost the guilt.

Mom's voice brought me back. "Something made me look for his map case this week. I opened it and found things in it … you should have."

She brought the case to me. "Maps, of course," she said, sorting through the case and pulling out a bundle of papers. Her voice was barely a whisper, "but also some photographs and a letter. It's for you, Sophie."

I took the bundled contents from her and sat in the one piece of furniture we had brought home with us from Ecuador. It was a sturdy Andes piece we called the "Papa chair" because Dad loved the lacquered wooden armrests and woven back. He always welcomed me into his lap. As a child I played near him for hours while he worked on flight plans, studied his worn black Spanish Bible, and met with local missionaries dispensing love and advice. I absorbed it all. I still have his Bible beside my bed as an unopened memory.

I untied the native twine holding the contents together and removed the brittle and yellowed maps. Below there was a damaged photo of me as a girl, still in pigtails, dwarfed in the large right-side pilot's seat of our parked airplane. Dad was behind the seat with his arms wrapped around me, guiding my hands to switches on the instrument panel.

I remembered the moment completely. Dad's old crew chief Pete had taken the photo. I looked up at Mom to explain. "I've got my eyes closed because Dad wanted me to be able to find important switches in the dark in case I couldn't see from the right seat." I should have been there to help. *Why was there no chance for me to help him, God?*

We sat simply looking at the old photograph together, the lost daughter and the widow.

I remembered exactly what it was like to feel his arms. I carefully picked out the letter addressed to me from among the other papers, keeping it closed. "Can I take the letter home, Mom? I can't read it now."

"Of course, darling. Call me after, if you want to talk."

I don't remember the drive home. My roommate, Darcy, was out when I got back so I had the apartment to myself. I changed into my softest pajamas and headed to my safe spot—my French queen bed. Resting my back against the grey upholstered headboard, I tucked my legs under the emerald duvet. Max, my Golden Retriever, immediately sensed I was upset. Opening the letter, I recognized my father's tight, controlled handwriting with the little figures and north star sketch he always drew of the two of us. Dad said the star stood for going after the 'highest goals that God has for us.'[1] Dad taught me the real stars, and in a pinch I can still use them in the dark to orient myself back toward home.

---

1   Jennings, Ken and Hyde, Heather, *The Greater Goal: Connecting Purpose and Performance* (San Francisco: Berrett-Koehler Publishers, Inc.), 2012.

A

RODNEY ALSAS

Sophie,

I wanted to pray together and say goodbye this morning but you were asleep. Pete is working out an electrical glitch on the airplane. You'll get this in the mail from the Andes so you should save the stamp.

I'm sorry about our fight last night. I love you. We were both being a little stubborn. Will you forgive me? I really don't like to be away from you and Mom, but we are making such a difference for kids in the mountains.

Here's a surprise I was going to tell you this morning. Mom and I decided that you are old enough to come with us to the interior on our next trip this summer. I know you've been wanting to come with us.

I hope your practice goes well today. Remember hija, nobody can ever make you quit.

I love you. Te quiero.

See you soon mi amor,
Dad

'See you soon,' he said.

But of course, he did not see me soon.

Tears pricked at my eyes, but I was not going to cry. Years later, this letter painted a picture of what my life could have been, me working in the mission field. What would he think of who I was now and of how far I had strayed? At least I'd tried to help people and communities. I hoped he couldn't see me. If he could think—wherever he was—let him just think of me as a girl in the foothills of the Andes.

Sleeping was out of the question. I chose my usual coping method, writing. If someone ever found my box of journals, they'd learn a lot about me. Many of my entries were addressed to God in both English and Spanish, but I doubted He listened.

That night I had another vivid nightmare. I was flying our old airplane through the Andes. But I was lost in the dark without a North Star or moon to guide me. I was sure that the dangerous rising terrain was all around me, but I couldn't see it.

INFILTRATING THE COMMUNITY

The next morning, I felt a kiss in my sleep.

It kept going and the kiss got wetter. I woke up to Max's slobbery tongue. "Gross, Max!"

I got up, wiping dog slobber off my face as I walked to the bathroom, where I scrubbed my face extra hard. I fixed a cup of green tea, hoping the caffeine would bring a bright start to my day. I put exactly thirteen fresh blueberries into my protein shake. It has to be an odd number because I have a problem.

Darcy had already left. She had a job out toward the airport working as a chemical engineer. She was brilliant—younger but a year ahead of me in school, and after graduating, got a competitive job with Bayer. I came to Pittsburgh and we became roommates. She helped me build my confidence. Mom helped me get into journalism.

Darcy introduced me to some of her outdoorsy, super-athletic friends who tried to drive me to be like them. They got me into high intensity training for a sprint triathlon, but I was still not so sure about that. Darcy was one of the most athletic, charismatic people on the planet. She balanced out my solid introversion. It was hard for me to meet people, especially that odd subspecies, men.

I stood in front of my closet and debated what to wear. I wanted professionalism, but this was a college ministry. I always have a hard time know what to wear to fit in. *What to do?* After several tries and a pile on the floor, I finally settled on a green silk shirt with white skinny jeans. With investigative walking in my future I picked sensible, not-so-attractive white tennis shoes to go with my outfit.

I looked in my floor-length mirror, ready to seize the day. "I've got a story," I said to Max, raising my hands over my head like a cheerleader. He refused to comment. "It might not be a challenging story, but it will be some good practice."

I spent the rest of the morning at home researching the leadership of The House, learning as much as I could. My mom was a terrific source, so I called her half a dozen times. One of my newspaper colleagues also knew the ministry and each of the leaders. She had been part of The House while studying at Carnegie Mellon, so I got the lowdown.

This group did look unique. They worked on—or, as my colleague said, "lived out"— a set of Christian community discipleship practices and were known for "applied practical Servant Leadership development." Even non-Christians came to their regular leadership development sessions that they held frequently on campus at The House.

The staff leaders in The House were a bit older than most undergrads and even some grad students. International students made up a significant demographic in the ministry, so one of the key leaders was an international post-grad student from China.

Finally ready to go, I took a clean notebook and three black pens, making sure I had my phone along for recording interviews. I took one last look in the mirror and repeated my own version of a confidence booster I'd used since college. "I've got a story, and I'm going to tell it!" This time Max woofed and wagged his tail in response this time. I love my dog.

I climbed into my bright yellow Jeep, 'Sam.' I could make out the Channel 11 logo on the side of the chopper flying overhead. "Bet they're on their way to another fire, Sam." Suspicious fires were the hot story in Pittsburgh. And yes, I talked to my dog and to my Jeep. What can I say, I'm quirky.

Not everyone was charmed. My last ex described me as "beautiful, broken, and baffling." He left because I was that girl that "no one could know." That hurt. If I was broken before, he managed to smash the pieces into a fine dust. That was nearly a year ago, and I'd been single ever since. I shifted my energy to my job, my collected menagerie of ethnic clothes, and high intensity workouts.

Sam hit a pothole crater, focusing me back on driving. The Jeep suspension was unbowed by Pittsburgh potholes and kept going—no problem. I reached The House in good time, leaving me five minutes to look over my notes on the leaders before I was due to meet them.

Luke Jarrell: Campus ministry leader and Servant Leader

- A Pittsburgh native, in his early thirties.

- Former top goalie on Michigan's hockey team. His junior year he had a rare goalie injury in a tournament championship game that was career-ending.

- He was a B/C student in his classes. He is still searching for identity post-hockey. Before he was a Christian who played hockey. Now he is just a Christian.

- While he apparently misses the hockey part of his identity, Luke has tried to move on. He did some sort of spiritual journey that helped focus his life. He leads the ministry at The House, providing steady, great leadership. He still wears hockey jerseys.

- Now taking seminary classes part-time in Pittsburgh. His folks live in town.

Jie 'Julie' Zheng: Post medical school fellow at Pitt. A doctor and very part-time House staff

- From a small village outside of Chengdu, in southwestern China.

- Described as brilliant, friendly, and mature beyond her years.

- Julie's parents wanted her to study something prestigious and she wanted to work with people. They agreed on medical school in the U.S. and Julie plans to return to work as a doctor in Chengdu.

- She became a Christian through the hospitality of The House. Her first encounter with The House was when they had their "Welcome to Pittsburgh" lunch especially aimed at international students.

– Kelsey, a former House leader, led Julie to Christ and took her under her wing. She regularly draws other international students into The House.

– She is looking forward to moving back to Chengdu to be able to help her family, practice medicine and share what she has learned about Christ. She's passionate about increasing access to health care especially for the frail and elderly, like her grandparents.

<u>Byron Dubois Washington:</u> Third generation army combat wounded veteran, African–American

– Larger than life. Byron's family lineage includes a Buffalo Soldier, a Tuskegee Airman, and three Vietnam Veterans. His mom is a veteran of the Gulf War, having served in the Navy on the USNS Comfort. His dad, though, is a pastor. Interesting.

– Grew up in rural Georgia. Was highly involved in the local Young Life Military Community Youth Ministry program. Planned on attending a historically black university but decided to serve after a friend was killed in a civilian terrorist attack.

- Served combat tours with a secretive special ops unit out of Fort Bragg, NC. Redacted records show he was assigned within JSOC. (What's that?)

- He was a combat medic, sort of like a military paramedic.

- Very highly decorated, earning a Silver Star for valor in Helmand Province. Treated in a series of military and VA hospitals, Byron deals with the physical and PTSD consequences of combat. That's what my coworker said.

- Took his GI Bill and finished a physiology degree at Pitt. He has seen a world his classmates can only begin to imagine.

- He is a super gregarious campus leader. He joined The House after being treated at the Pittsburgh VA hospital.

I got out of Sam-the-Jeep and walked up to the sprawling, beautiful stone mansion just off Fifth Avenue. It was a dramatic building, scrubbed clean of all the soot that paints many of the mansions that have been standing since Pittsburgh's smoggy steel years.

THE HOUSE

uke Jarrell, the leader of The House, was waiting for me just inside the massive oak front door. He greeted me with a broad smile. He wanted to give me a hug, but I demurred, eager to remain professional. Despite his somewhat hefty build, no doubt compounded by a lack of hockey workouts, Luke moved like a cat. He had a stylish scruff of beard, and his brown oval glasses rested on a nose that had been broken more than once. We got coffee from the kitchen, and Luke directed us back into the expansive main living room.

On our way, we passed a room off the kitchen that held a long, medieval-looking table with carved legs and metal bonding around the top. The imposing piece seemed out of place with contemporary college life. Luke saw me looking and joked, "Since this place is called The House, we call that 'The Table.' It's sort of a joke. We also have 'The Cat' around here somewhere."

"I have a dog at home."

Luke's distinct Pittsburgh accent meant that he tended to draw out his 'o' vowels making them into an 'ahh' sound so as he spoke, 'house' became 'haus.' He was what locals called themselves: a Yinzer, from the Pittsburgh slang *yinz,* or "you all." A hundred disparate ethnic groups had come together to forge steel and create this one-of-a-kind dialect. I knew lots of those groups from my community work. I still had a lot of friends out there.

We continued to the main room where two large windows let in the natural light. The adjacent wall had a huge stone and tile fireplace surrounded by built-in bookshelves. The original wooden floor was restored to a warm pecan glow. In contrast, college student tested furniture occupied much of the room. I grabbed a spot on a faded blue couch after glancing to make sure there wasn't anything weird on it, remembering my own student furniture.

Luke settled into an overstuffed cracked leather chair across from me, and I dove right into the interview. I'm often underestimated because I look so young, and I thought a brisk pace would drive home the point that I was a real reporter on assignment. I opened my oblong notebook — reporter's notebooks are traditionally long and thin, originally designed to fit in a man's shirt pocket — and pulled out a pen, which of course didn't work. I went to my backup. Dad taught me to always have a backup. *Thanks, Padre.*

"My editor told me that the hidden secrets of The House are contained in this mysterious House mantra." I handed Luke the paper from Ben.

See Differently – Serve Differently

He snorted a laugh. "Sophie, I bet you didn't know that Ben spent his four years at CMU practically living here in The House. Don't let him fool you, he knows all about this."

The conspiracy deepened. "He didn't mention it."

"We love Ben. We're happy to help you with 'See Differently and Serve Differently.' It's the Applied Servant Leadership framework we use here on campus and out in the community as we do our discipleship work."

I doodled.

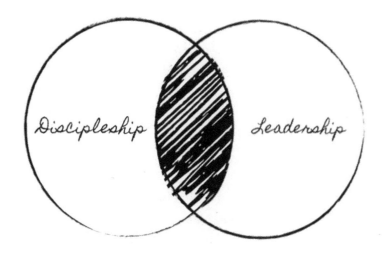

"We believe how we choose to serve and lead comes from how we see people and God differently. You will get to know this all for yourself."

"That's why I'm here, Luke. Tell me about the alumni of The House?" I took a sip of coffee. Burnt! Growing up in the Andes on excellent coffee every day made me a snob, but I was raised not to complain about what people offered.

"Alumni of The House go everywhere. We want to equip them as servant leaders to better do what God calls them to do. Our spiritual and physical community continues to be a source of encouragement and growth to alumni in their day-to-day lives. God calls us all to do good work in His great kingdom.

We do our work as Jesus would do it if He were in our job. Every job can be done with God and for others."[2]

"Our work is to join God in forming disciples who will serve well everywhere in God's great kingdom."[3] He paused and let me catch up on my notes. Over his head I spied a placard of sorts. It said:

See Differently
God & People

Serve Differently
Way Power
Why Power

It was the T-shirt slogan with a bit more added.

Just then, a young Asian woman walked through the arched doorway. Luke said, "Let's meet the team."

---

2   Willard, Dallas, *Personal lecture* (Renovaré Institute, Chicago, IL), 2009.

3   John Stahl-Wert. *With: A True Story* (Pittsburgh, PA: Steelworth Press), 2008.

IN TRAINING FOR REIGNING

Luke introduced me: "Sophie, meet Julie Zheng, our resident doctor."

Julie, who had a silver and pink stethoscope looped around her neck, was wearing a white lab coat over her skinny jeans and bright red blouse. I was envious. With my copper hair, I could never pull off red.

Julie walked around the table, her slight arms full of heavy medical books. Right behind her was a powerfully built African-American man in a gray Pitt sweatshirt and khakis. His hair was cut in a military fade with flecks of premature gray and white. He had a well-worn black backpack with military patches slung over his broad shoulders.

I stood up and stuck my hand out. "Sophie Alsas. I'm a reporter from the *Herald,* doing a story on The House."

"We know," he boomed, a grin spreading across his face. "We're going to be famous!" Julie hit him hard on the shoulder and smiled. Her punch did not even register.

"I'm Julie." Firm grip, eye-to-eye contact, and a sunny smile. She continued, "I'm a surgical fellow at Pitt. We use the See Differently - Serve Differently principles you will see at The House at our hospital. Come and see."

Byron rocked back and forth on his feet. The sway was unnatural. I could see metal and plastic where a sock should have been, a prosthetic. *Do your research, Sophie!* The guy was a combat wounded veteran, I should have known about his injury. His face told a further story. His dark skin was pebbled with dozens of patches of scar tissue, a virtual constellation.

"Yinz guys want to join us?" Luke invited them both.

"I'd appreciate anything you all would like to add," I said.

Byron took that in, seemed to consider it, and said, "Hold that thought." He wheeled around and limped out of the room.

Taking a seat on the couch, the rest of us watched him go.

"Byron's in some discomfort today," Julie said. "We should pray for him."

We all looked at the door. "I've got a little time before my clinic," Julie continued, and then she repeated Luke's line: "I'm so glad *you're* doing our story. We love your mom. She's been down here helping and talks about you a lot."

Julie looked at the door again. "Can you hold on a second? Let me just check on Byron." She walked briskly out of the room.

Luke filled in. "There's one other key leader, Jeb Phelps, who leads in our sister community house. I want you to meet him. His work is also around discipleship, but in a work setting."

The other House? I pressed on.

"Can you give me your definition of discipleship here at The House? I need to use your working definition in my article."

"Sure. We help Christ's followers to do all that Jesus said to do and did himself. We show love and serve students to help them grow deeper in their relationship with Christ. God calls all of us to join Him in achieving good and great goals together.

"I once heard Dallas Willard say, 'We've already started an eternal kind of life. You can learn to truly see His Kingdom in action now. We're all here in *training for reigning*.'[4] We're learning and developing the character we need to join Christ in leading and stewarding his kingdom starting now, and ... well ... forever. We're here to grow as disciples, to serve others, and to learn to lead with a servant heart."

We're all here in *training for reigning*. We're learning and developing the character we need to join Christ in leading and stewarding his kingdom starting now, and ... well ... forever.

While we were talking, Julie slipped back onto the couch beside me. Byron was right behind her. He walked over to the fireplace mantel behind us and struck a match, lighting a white candle. We watched as it sputtered.

"What's with that?"

Byron picked up the candle like he was doing this little demonstration. "It's a House tradition. The church worships in some dark places. In a most real way, we're downrange in enemy territory, and candles push back the darkness. It helps us to see."

Luke laughed. "Byron has given out hundreds of those candles. I think he believes we should be ready for some long, lights-out national emergency. Maybe it's the medic in him."

Byron just lifted the candle up for us to see. He explained, "Some nuns in Eastern Pennsylvania make these candles for us." The hot wax dripped onto his hand, but he did not flinch.

---

4   Willard. *Personal lecture*, 2009.

He said, "Candles also remind us to see differently. At The House, we believe that leading others starts with seeing both God and people differently. Many of us are trapped into seeing God as a grumpy judge or an absent parent. Actually, God absolutely loves us, enjoys us, and desires to have a personal relationship with us. His deepest desire is for us to live, love, and partner with Him in His work of bringing light into our dark world. He's with us to give us strength for our daily work, friends to join us, and people to love right in front of us. We believe God always has our highest good in mind. In fact, He knows what's best for us, even more than we do. What many people consider to be "rules for Christian behavior," we see as loving boundaries He has set so we can fully become who He created us to be. Ultimately, we trust God's heart for us. We learn to think and see that way. This seeing reality is at the center of what The House is. We help our students to see God as on their side, loving, joyful, and for us in all we do in His kingdom."

"How does seeing God differently affect how you lead?"

"When we see God truly for who He is, the most loving and giving being in the universe, we can also happily join Him in enjoying and leading His Kingdom. We're on an adventure. An eternal kind of life starts here, right at The House, right on planet Earth. It's an adventure to bring light into the darkness, to overcome evil and injustice with good, to reflect His image, and be His hands and feet.

"I know that's a lot Sophie, and I'm getting hot wax on my fingers. Yow!"

We all laughed. Luke said, "We prepared some background for you on The House's applied servant leadership principles." They went to the kitchen for more coffee and to let me read.

See Differently – God

We practice an applied form of Servant Leadership at The House. What appeals to us, what first sets this form of leading apart, is learning to see what is true and real.

Start with God.

Some of us see Him as a distant, harsh judge or an absent parent. Actually, He is wildly loving towards us, wholly for us, and deeply relational. The forever relationship mending work of Jesus the Christ makes this real. God dances for joy at our restored relationship. He watches us, not looking for ways to punish but keeping His eyes on us for the same reasons that any loving parents watches their child. God wants to be with us and for us. God is working to form us with the character of Jesus and to empower us to join Him in co-managing His Kingdom. We join Him as a fellow servant.

"Instead, whoever wants to become great among you must be your servant, and whoever wants to be first must be slave of all. For even the Son of Man did not come to be served, but to serve, and to give his life as a ransom for many," Mark 10:43-45.

See Differently – People

How we best live and lead is made possible by how we see others. Do we see people as objects to be used for our benefit? Or do we see others as worthy individuals stamped with God's marks of endearment? The question is: Do we see people the way God sees people?

People are eternal, never- ending creatures made in God's own image.

If God sees the people around us as worthy, so should we.

People are full of God-given strengths --- bring out the best in them.

People are ready for great adventures — invite them.

People are sometimes offensive — love them.

People get lost — find them. Invite them home.

People flourish with good leadership — empower them to overcome evil with good in God's never- ending Kingdom, starting now.

Seeing God rightly and seeing people clearly helps us to serve well!

Serve Differently

We strive to lead others with respect. We practice everyday love. We serve by making a 'way' for them to succeed. We connect our team to the 'why' of their efforts.

Way Power-As servant leaders, we put ourselves in service to those who work with and for us, encouraging and empowering them to grow and perform against our shared goals. We dedicate ourselves to discerning best routes forward, building teams capable of drawing on each other's strengths and abilities, leveraging our available assets, building on past successes, creating cultures of shared achievement, giving rich feedback and coaching for success. We celebrate successes and model ourselves to be proactive people, outcome achieving, reliable, and trustworthy. In short we commit to having the kind of character that is crucial to community harmony and success.

Why Power-As servant leaders, we put ourselves in service to the purpose or cause that calls us to give our very best. We work to create connections from every person on our team to the highest and best greater goals that achieve good for those we serve, including ourselves. We work to connect all of us to doing the good that is out *in front* of us, *beside us* with our honored colleagues, and *within us* as that person whom God loves and sacrificed for. We aim to create lines of hope and optimism as we see the progress we all make against our most precious shared greater goals.

The team filtered back in.

"Can you give me an example of how you 'see others differently'?" I asked.

"Ah," Luke said. "There's the listening booth. We do it weekly in one of the quads on campus. One of the best ways to see people differently is to really listen to them, to hear their stories: their hurts, aspirations, successes, despair, and journey so far. We started setting up a listening booth in the quads a year ago, and it is one of the best things we have ever done.

"The listening booth was set up as an experiment — not a booth, technically, but a three-sided tent with tea, Cokes, a couple of chairs, and a couch. A small sign says, 'We'll talk with you about anything. We're pretty good listeners at The

House.' Most of us did not expect much, but word spread that we were genuinely interested in what people had to say. We weren't preaching. We were interesting people who did not judge. Students started coming. Most days, there is a line."

"What do you hear?" I asked.

They traded comments:

My Mom and Dad never listened.

I suck at life.

I'm lonely.

My friends are on Instagram, not real life.

Will God forgive me?

I repeat the same awful sins over and over.

I had a terrible father. He abused me. Help me understand God as a 'father.'

"Students sometimes wait hours to be heard," Luke said. "Some make their way to The House and stick around.

"We listened, got good at it, and were forever changed in how we saw the students. This is 'See Differently' thinking in action."

Byron added, "The ministry team began listening sessions for each other. We began to see each other differently. We better saw needs, heart, aspirations, pains, weakness, and broken places. We were able to love better and serve better as a team.

"Sophie, we hope you will see how The House alumni serve differently because they see differently. We will be visiting some sites with you to see the deeper heart attitudes of Seeing and Serving Differently put into action. **It's not about techniques, it's about a more fundamental change inside that enables one to see and lead differently.**"

It's not about techniques, it's about a more fundamental change inside that enables one to see and lead differently.

Luke finished the thought. "I hope you will observe all of this here. At The House we learn to see the good, the abilities and the potential in our teammates. I loved that in hockey and I love it here."

Byron and Julie burst out laughing and checked their watches together. "What?" I cocked my head to the side, puzzled.

Byron explained, "It usually only takes Luke a couple of minutes to work hockey into any conversation. Julie and I had a bet on how long it would take."

Luke just glared over his glasses at his teammates, and said, "Moving on."

I liked these guys.

"How would a servant leader build and help teams succeed? How would it be different from other team approaches?" I asked.

Luke answered, "The fundamentals of good teams are the same. Purpose, build on strengths, trust and practice." He laughed. "Yes, I saw the basics put to work in hockey. But there are distinctions to working in teams of servant leaders. We see the strengths individuals bring to a team, and we draw on them. We know how we can complement each other, and we practice it. We learn to give each other tough love feedback, serving to help one another succeed. And we always look for the path that God already laid out for us to succeed — that's part of the way power."

I learned enough from this start to write a whole article. Building teams from an applied servant leadership perspective was good. It dawned on me that I recognized every one of them from the way Ben ran our newsroom. Now I know where he got the approach. The practices flowed from the 'See Differently - Serve Differently' principles applied to teams.

- See teammates as honored, eternally growing, legitimate partners in pursuit of good for the world. It's an adventure!
- The performance, achievements and goals are important, but the highest payoff is to build each other up. People were the ones for whom Christ died.
- The applied practices of forgiveness, mercy, love, second chances, building each other up, patience, compassionate presence, and humility are made into team 'ways.' That's what they mean by 'way power.' They are very practical tools to run team meetings and achieve together. The House alumni are using the tools they learned at The House in every imaginable business, non-profit, government and entrepreneurial organization in the country. They were making practices of the heart into practices of the team.

  If a teammate has a blind spot, help them see.
  If a teammate has offended you, seek understanding and reconciliation.
  If a teammate needs help, help them and coach them.
  When the team experiences setbacks, understand them at a cause-effect level and put in place better ways of working. They use 'After Action Reviews.'

After-Action Review

An asset based approach that builds on both successes and failures for continuous improvement

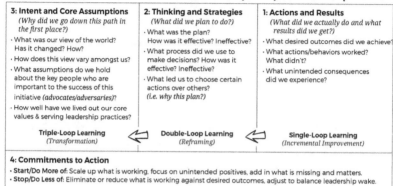

3: Intent and Core Assumptions	2: Thinking and Strategies	1: Actions and Results
(Why did we go down this path in the first place?)	*(What did we plan to do?)*	*(What did we actually do and what results did we get?)*
· What was our view of the world? Has it changed? How?	· What was the plan? How was it effective? Ineffective?	· What desired outcomes did we achieve?
· How does this view vary amongst us?	· What process did we use to make decisions? How was it effective? Ineffective?	· What actions/behaviors worked? What didn't?
· What assumptions do we hold about the key people who are important to the success of this initiative *(advocates/adversaries)*?	· What led us to choose certain actions over others? *(i.e. why this plan?)*	· What unintended consequences did we experience?
· How well have we lived out our core values & serving leadership practices?		

| **Triple-Loop Learning** *(Transformation)* | ⇦ | **Double-Loop Learning** *(Reframing)* | ⇦ | **Single-Loop Learning** *(Incremental Improvement)* |

4: Commitments to Action
· **Start/Do More of:** Scale up what is working, focus on unintended positives, add in what is missing and matters.
· **Stop/Do Less of:** Eliminate or reduce what is working against desired outcomes, adjust to balance leadership wake.

Adapted from: Learning in the Thick of It, Marilyn Darling, Charles Parry and Joseph Moore, Harvard Business Review, July 2005 and Action Inquiry: The Secret of Timely and Transforming Leadership, Bill Torbert, Dalmar Fisher, David Rooke, 2004

- When the team experiences success, especially unexpected success, understand the reasons why and seek to advance that success at a larger scale and speed.

- Create a culture of rich feedback to each other. Keep promises to each other. Connect everyone's work directly to the customer's experience; this creates significance in daily work. This is the 'why' of why we do our work. That's 'why power.'

- Take time to both measure progress and process the real meaning of that progress. Credit the team as a whole publicly. Correct in private, with empathy and coaching.

- Learn from mistakes 'of the head.' Mistakes 'of the heart,' ethical and/or intentionally hurtful mistakes, deserve a different level of attention.

- Apply 'seeing others with love and serving them with their best in mind.' This may even mean letting teammates experience negative consequences. It certainly means encouragement and coaching. Celebrate learning, teamness, and success.

"So does The House do other things? I thought campus ministries were known for being fun," I said.

"Hey," Luke amended, "The House also does normal fun college things. We eat together, watch Pittsburgh sports, and do life together. Yes, we watch hockey. I'm a big Michigan fan. There are Ohio State fans also in The House. We see them as brothers and sisters, except maybe a few days a year. That's when the schools play each other in football, hockey, or basketball."

Julie leaned over to me. "You're invited to come closer, Sophie. Why don't you come tonight for our community dinner as Byron's and my guest? We're on host duty together." The two high-fived each other. They moved their hands away slowly. I noted the micro-signals of a connection.

"Sure!"

I drove Sam-the-Jeep home reflecting on my unwanted re-entry into Christianity. When I got back, my roommate was cooking to loud electric salsa music and doing her 'Darcy happy dance.' We are so different.

"How'd the interview go?" she called out over her music and sizzling food.

"It was a good start. What are you cooking? It smells wonderful."

She stirred vigorously, wafting the smell in my direction.

"I'm doing South American. Your kind of food, chica. Want some?"

"I would, but I'm actually going back to The House tonight for a community dinner. Want to come with?" I depend on

Darcy in social situations. She shines in the spotlight, while I try to fade into the background.

"Nah, I can't, but it sounds like the interviews went well if they want you to come back so soon. I was planning on going to the gym and climbing. Maybe I can stop by after."

Darcy took the pan off the stove and tossed the food into a bowl. Max gave a small whine and looked up at us with his irresistible eyes.

"Fine, fine," Darcy said, tossing a chunk of chicken, which Max caught in the air.

"Okay girly," Darcy grabbed her bowl and walked toward her bedroom. "I'm gonna eat this and hit the gym. Text me the address of this place and I'll swing by after."

"Thanks, I will. Have fun bouldering."

That evening Sam-the-Jeep got me back to The House later than I'd hoped. I'm not a very punctual person. I took in my destination as I pulled up. The House was almost glowing from the inside. Byron's candles graced windows at every level. It had been one of Pittsburgh's great homes from the first golden era of the city: the days of Carnegie, Mellon, Heinz, and Westinghouse, steel barons with a legacy to protect. There were still a few of these classic old mansions around, mostly repurposed. The House was donated to the ministry ages ago. A campus and tech cluster had grown up around it. It was pitch-black tonight in Pittsburgh, no moon or stars. The House was resisting the darkness.

FIREFIGHTER

The House was packed—noisy and buzzing. I walked in trying to memorize the scene. The students were all types— jocks, nerds, internationals, preps and steampunks. Julie took my arm and introduced me all around, sliding me into the pulsing community as if I were a member, not a reporter. I heard conversations about typical student stuff mixed with uniquely Christian talk. My ears were adjusting as I eased back into a setting of believers.

I spotted Byron as he ambled over to greet a couple of guys. He hugged them and then punched one of them in the chest playfully, but pretty hard. One of Byron's friends was wiry and thin, dressed in a dirt- and sweat-stained shirt and athletic shorts. But his other friend really drew my attention: Tall and built, his light blue polo showed off a tan, muscular upper body and short brown hair. Maybe an athlete?

"Who is Byron talking to?" I asked Julie.

"Those are some of the guys from Byron's accountability group — Matt Cummings and the community staff leader Luke mentioned, Jeb Phelps. Matt plays soccer for Pitt and it looks like he just came from practice. I think Jeb came from work." I was staring.

To my horror, Byron looked up just then and called me over. "Hey Sophie, these are some people I want you to meet."

I tried to walk over to the group gracefully. As I approached, I heard Jeb talking with an accent I'd heard a lot in Pittsburgh — West Virginian, maybe?

"Guys, I want you to meet Sophie Alsas. She's a reporter who is doing a story on The House."

The wiry one stuck out his hand, allowing me a whiff of sweat and sunscreen. "Hi, I'm Matt." Reading my distance, he apologized. "Sorry, I just got out of practice."

"Matt's a senior this year. He's one of the co-captains of Pitt's soccer team," Byron clued me in.

The tall guy was next. Up close, he was even more impressive.

"Hi, I'm Jeb," he said, giving a slight nod of his head. He had a wrap and bandage on one hand and a glass in the other, so he couldn't shake.

"Beer?" I asked.

"Close. It's root beer. I don't drink anymore. There's all kinds of pop in the fridge if you want some," Jeb's deep, resonating voice mesmerized me.

"Well, I'm going to go grab something. Do you want anything at all, Sophie?" Matt peeled away, his lengthy strides taking him and his dust cloud to the kitchen.

"Root beer?" I sailed the words after him.

"I'll come with you," Byron called out, following Matt's trail.

That left me and Jeb Phelps together in awkward silence. Too bad Darcy wasn't here, she would know what to do. I had to think of something to say, I was not ready to let him go. I did my best to channel my inner Darcy.

"How do you guys know each other?" I asked, lamely.

"Matt and I were roommates when he was a freshman and I was a sophomore. Believe me, tonight isn't the worst he's smelled." I made a face, and he laughed.

"So how'd you meet Byron then?"

"Matt and I ran into Byron out at Schenley Plaza. We all threw the football around for a bit and he invited us to The House for dinner. That was three years ago, and we've been coming ever since. Byron's now my best friend. I guess we're on staff together, him on campus and me in the other House."

Bingo! This is the guy from the second, mysterious house. Lucky me!

Jeb continued. "You know, Byron was a combat medic before he became a ministry leader and part-time paramedic. He now brings that veteran experience to us at the fire department."

I felt a sudden panic. "What do you mean *us* at the fire department? Aren't you a student?"

"Nope, I'm a fireman. I finished two years before I dropped out of Pitt, completed my fire academy training, and got the job. I decided that if I couldn't commit to a major I might as well make a difference, so now I'm a firefighter out of Station 9. We keep busy, especially now with this cluster of city fires."

I could not believe it. *Come on, God!*

"Really?" I said weakly.

"Not impressed?"

"I totally hate fires," I said.

"Fires happen, but then we go to work. You know, saving lives, protecting the community." He smiled, peeling back my resolve by a fraction. "It can be exciting."

"You could die," I said bluntly.

"Nope, that's not in the job description," Jeb replied. "Saving people is what I do. Besides, Christians will never die, at least not as we commonly think of it. We're already 'never-ending spiritual beings,' as Byron says."

That was not the answer I wanted. I tried to stop my hands from shaking.

"You Christians can be so wrong and believe you're right." I was possibly talking to my dead father who left me. "I'm sorry. This isn't about you. There's a backstory." I attempted a smile to soften my words. *Way to kill the mood, Sophie.*

Then this fireman rescued me.

"Hey, wanna get some of the 'Burgh's best ice cream later? Byron and I were thinking of heading over to Dave and Andy's after this. It's down in the middle of Pitt's campus."

"Sure," another voice answered for me. Darcy had arrived behind me, and just in time!

The ice cream at Dave and Andy's was great. To my utter dread, I found I was quickly interested in Jeb. He was kind to everyone and I was pulled into his magnetic field. This was a bad scenario. Therapy point maybe, because I lost my dad so painfully I resist the possibility of a real relationship. Despite that, the evening was great. Practically the whole shop was listening as Jeb, Byron, and Darcy did their extrovert thing, laughing and involving everyone around them in the fun. I did my best to keep up with them.

The guys took a break at one point, and Darcy and I talked a bit off to one side. Darcy was pretty observant and direct, so before I could even say anything she commented, "You should be careful with Jeb." She knew me well enough to see that I was interested, but also knew I was self-destructive in relationships.

I tried weakly to counter her. "Well, Darcy, Jeb works in a firehouse that looks like it's in the middle of the mystery fires.

That's a real story. He's in the other House, so professionally I'm obligated."

She frowned, "Riiight… I say no!"

The guys finally came back, and they had a plan. Jeb made the offer.

"Hey, since you're going to learn about all of us, why don't you start at the firehouse?"

Darcy and I exchanged looks.

"I'll come," I said, to both my and Darcy's surprise. Darcy gave me a look but kept quiet.

"Great!" Jeb and Byron smiled and exclaimed simultaneously. They actually high-fived each other. Weird.

The shop was closing, and we pushed out onto the still busy campus street. Students parted around us like a stream around stones. Darcy turned to me, hands on her hips.

"You're crazy, girl."

Darcy turned and kept walking. I hoped that tomorrow I would be as ready as I pretended to be just now.

Back at home I walked Max and talked to him about my adventures. I talked to him about Jeb and the bigger than life ex-soldier Byron. And I wondered what his time in the military was like.

AFGHANISTAN

June 10, Just outside of Deh Dala.

Sgt. Byron Washington tried hard to imagine what this place was really like in peaceful, happier times.

Dust whirled around the landing zone as the CH-47 set down, where ten pairs of boots marched off it. *Ranger school was hard, medic training was hard, but this new unit was very hard.* It took over a year of tough work just to get invited in.

Byron Dubois Washington, future campus minister, had been sent with his team from Jalalabad Air Base to a smaller forward deployed combat outpost— "COP" to those who would be manning it—called COP Gutierrez. His unit would be there for a few critical missions supporting some of his old Ranger friends.

"That it over there?" Byron asked his squad leader, nodding to a long perimeter fence that was dotted with a number of guard towers. The whole thing couldn't have been more than a half mile across.

"Must be," said Staff Sergeant Messina. "Not much else around here. Bad guys everywhere, though." They were lightly manned and in deep as usual.

Byron grunted in agreement. Then he added: "But we're also surrounded by helpers." Byron was famous for positive, cryptic sayings.

It was about a five-minute walk from the landing site to the perimeter of the COP, and the squad was greeted by a pair of young privates, vigilantly standing guard. The members of the squad each pulled out their IDs and, when cleared, were motioned in past the perimeter. Security was easier in these smaller outposts when compared to the monstrosities of larger Main Operating Bases—but the tradeoff was that there were a lot less facilities. There was a makeshift clinic that had been set up months before, but nothing that could be called a working hospital. So Byron, as the squad's medic, was going to be pushed to the limits of his capability, and he could already feel the stress mounting.

August 24, and dozens of ops later...

"Three Strykers on the whole COP and we bring the one that's prone to breakdowns," Nikovski shouted in his fading Brooklyn accent. He jumped out of the M1126 Infantry Carrier Vehicle, where the other members of his squad still waited, kicked one of the huge tires, and immediately lit a smoke. "Woulda been better off walking in the first place," he mumbled through the cigarette. The "clink" of his lighter snapping shut seemed to punctuate his point.

It had been early evening when they went out on their mission, and it was coming up on midnight already. The good news was that there wasn't a whole lot between COP Gutierrez and the nearby village of Deh Bala. The bad news was that there was a reason they used the heavily armored Strykers as transportation.

"It's fine," Messina retorted. "It's breathing in a lot of dust. Probably just needs a filter change or something."

Nikovski looked up from his cigarette. "You don't know anything about vehicle maintenance, do you?"

Messina shrugged.

Byron Washington was working away from his unit for a few days. He had tinkered extensively with his truck before joining the Army, and knew that there was a lot that could go wrong with any complex piece of machinery—especially one as complex as the Stryker. Clocking in at just over sixteen tons, it was a behemoth of a vehicle: eight wheels, a hull made of hard steel plating, a big diesel engine, and an M240 machine gun for good measure.

But every piece of equipment in or on the Stryker represented a potential problem when it broke down.

"Someone radio the motor pool," Messina said, "and tell them we had another breakdown."

Collins, the squad's communications guy, still had his ear buds in and was listening to music. When he saw Messina looking at him, he pulled out one ear bud and asked, "Huh?"

The sounds of loud metal music blared from the hanging earbud.

"Nice of you to join us," Messina said with a smirk. "I said someone should radio the motor pool and tell them we had a breakdown. Did you not notice we stopped moving?"

"Oh, no, I noticed," Collins said as he bent down to the faceplate of the programmable PRC-117 radio and began punching in numbers. "I'm just frustrated." He finished programming the frequency in and moved back into his seat.

"All yours, boss," he said as he placed the loose earbud back in with a smile.

Byron knew that they probably weren't in any danger, but he said a silent prayer anyway. He must have been moving his lips unconsciously along with the words because another man in the unit, Campagnale, seemed to notice.

"Prayin', Washington?" he asked. The big Italian with a round face and dark brown hair was looking at him skeptically.

Byron smiled and laughed. "You know it. Just keepin' my man Jesus apprised of the situation."

"Hey, whatever works for you," Campagnale said with a shake of his head. But then he smiled. "If it gets us back in one piece, keep it up. Say one for me."

Messina's voice rose above their chatter.

"Two hours?" he said, nearly shouting, into the mic. "We're fifteen minutes away! What's gonna take so long?"

The reply on the other end was inaudible, going straight into Messina's headset, but it was clear that he didn't like it.

"Copy. Out," he said, tearing off his headset and throwing it on the ground in frustration.

"What's up?" Camagnale asked.

"No one's around," he answered, rubbing his eyes in frustration. "They have one guy manning the radio while the other two are out taking care of maintenance issues. He doesn't expect them back for at least another hour and a half."

"So," piped up Collins, who had taken out his earbuds when Messina threw his headset, "we just wait?"

Messina raised his eyebrows and put on a faux smile. "We wait."

And whatever Collins had said next was cut off—cut off by an explosion that sent dirt, debris, and shrapnel flying.

Byron's eyes immediately went outside the Stryker, to where Nikovski had been standing. And, just as his lips moved reflexively again in prayer, so did his body move reflexively in action. Before he could even realize what he was doing, he was moving to shield his friend with his body while scanning the area for threats.

Nikovski was laying on his back, eyes wide open in shock. Fortunately, he'd been wearing his body armor, and the heavy kevlar plates had absorbed some of the blast and debris. But as explosions — even a small one — could have traumatic effects both mentally and physically on the individual who experienced them.

Byron felt the hand of Messina on his shoulder as he heard him say, "Get him inside. Odds are good that they'll follow that up with another one."

Byron nodded and looked down. "Marko," he said sharply. "You good? Can you move?"

Nikovski blinked a few times, still in shock from the initial explosion, which looked like it had missed him by a few meters. It wasn't big enough to have been a rocket attack, so it was most likely a mortar. Not the most accurate of ordnance, but it could still do some damage.

"Yeah. I think so," he said in a daze. There was blood on his face, and it looked like he'd caught some shrapnel around the body armor. There was no evidence of a spinal injury, so Byron opted to get him out of harm's way immediately. Decision making and saving was what he did best.

"I'll take a look at you inside," he said as he helped his friend to his feet.

Messina was looking through the holographic sights of his high tech rifle, scanning the area for follow-up fire or any other threats. When he didn't see any, he backed in and closed the door to the Stryker.

Byron had Nikovski laid down on the steel floor of the vehicle and started to work on him. It wasn't exactly sterile hospital conditions, but it would have to do.

"Collins," Messina said, "radio the TOC and let them know what's going on. Washington, do your medic thing."

The Tactical Operations Center, basically where their squad called home, was where the rest of their leadership would be hanging out, monitoring the radios and planning for future missions. Byron nodded and got to work.

September 16

The inside of the Dragon dining facility—really just two big alaska tents with a chow line—was about thirty degrees cooler than the sweltering heat of eastern Afghanistan, and Byron was happy to be in it. He could tell by the smell that they were doing omelettes for breakfast today, and his stomach growled at the thought. Looking to his left at the rows of tables, he saw a familiar smiling face looking back at him.

"Marko!" Byron shouted from across the DFAC. "They let you out in public?"

The black-haired young man stood up and grinned, holding out his arms to display his lack of holes. "Good to get back in the fight. You did a good job of patching me up. They're not gonna have to evac me out; second Purple Heart though. Ha!" he exclaimed.

"Glad to hear it, brother," Byron said as he walked over and embraced his friend and squadmate. "I never stopped praying for you."

Nikovski waved it off. "I didn't ask you to."

"Well too bad, 'cause I did it anyway. You're not gonna tie a fighter's hands behind his back during a championship bout, are you? Once I did all I could, it was in God's hands."

Nikovski conceded the point. "You never stop, do you? Even in a place like this you find a way to believe."

"Especially here, and anyway, it's who I am," said Byron with his famous broad smile.

"Well, if you ever decide to leave this exciting line of work," Nikovski said as he gathered his things to go, "I'm sure some extra exciting ministry somewhere could use someone like you."

Their Unit commander, 'Dog' Butler, stepping into the room. He had that extra-serious game face on. "Gear up. Change of plans. We're linking up tonight back with some friendlies for an urban op. Bad news is that the hard-core guys we are after might be expecting us."

A helicopter ride later, the foreign spec ops and intel personnel were waiting out in the open to meet their partners, the U.S. operators. They were 'in the dark' about the American operators. All they knew was these Americans were elite, secretive, and veterans of countless fights. The foreign commander spotted the lead American soldier, carrying extra medic gear. He tried his best American slang.

"Who are you guys?" the foreign commander asked. He did not expect a reply. None was given.

Byron Dubois Washington, before the events that would turn him to campus ministry, knelt down and took off his night vision goggles, moving his right hand off his M4 rifle and cradling it with his left. His breathing was heavy and forced. The forty pounds of gear on his back wasn't doing him any favors. Wiping some of the sweat off his forehead, he looked up to see the squad leader, Sergeant Aguirre, who had been following closely behind, standing next to him. The foreign spec ops fell in behind them.

"Here should be fine," came the crackle over the radio. "Two minutes, then we move."

"Shouldn't be that much longer," Aguirre said with a grin that Byron could almost hear.

"Checkpoint's just up ahead. Just about a half a klick or so."

"Copy," Byron said between breaths. "Just fixing my nogs—they're a little busted up; I need my night vision."

He took off the NVG mount attached to his helmet and adjusted some settings, taking a moment to look around and regain his bearings. Without the green light of the goggles, Byron looked up to see pinpoints of starlight dotting the nighttime Mosul sky. Their small unit had been active in this area for a few months now, mostly going after high value targets that the Rangers couldn't, and by now Byron felt like he knew each road and alley by heart. The ones that they frequented the most were given names after things that reminded them of home: Supply Route Orlando, or Highway Chicago. Right now, they were on Main Route Dallas, which intersected with Route Cleveland; Cleveland would take them the rest of the way to the checkpoint.

"Right," Aguirre said. "Well, we gotta have our 'miracle medic' in working condition. The Unit needs you. We can hang here for a few and catch our breath." Aguirre continued to talk, "These are real bad guys we're after. They use every trick in the book to trap, ambush, and kill Americans. They've been killing and kidnapping village heads and even wives and kids who mostly just wanna live in peace. I believe in evil now."

Byron heard Aguirre key the mic on his radio and confirm the order to halt. At night, they usually kept their communications quiet. Their earpieces made it sound like Aguirre was right next to him.

Martinez, the squad's communications guy, walked over to Byron as he relaxed his rifle, letting it hang loose in its sling in front of his body armor. In the dark, everyone looks the same in tactical gear, but Byron knew it was him by the way that he walked: confident, and with just the right amount of swagger.

Martinez was a smoker — the rest of the squad regularly gave him grief for it — but the light discipline they were operating under for this mission meant that he couldn't light up. A cigarette at night was like sending off a flare to anyone who might be watching. Byron heard him take out the plastic dip can and put a chunk in his mouth, the strong scent of tobacco wafting over.

"What's the matter, Washington? You not getting enough cardio in?"

Byron finished his NVG adjustments and put them back on, looking up through their green lights to see the grin plastered across Martinez's face and a big bulge in his bottom lip.

"Funny," he retorted. "Just adjusting the focus." Under his breath, he added, "And you know I'm up for a footrace any time you are, old man."

Martinez chuckled. He was three weeks older than Byron, and they found out that the two of them had enlisted during the same week. Byron took every opportunity to remind him that Martinez was "the old friend."

"After we get back then, young soldier." He turned his head and spit, watching the Iraqi dirt absorb the moisture in seconds.

Standing back up, Byron took his rifle in both hands again, holding his finger just off the trigger guard and letting it rest against the front plate of his body armor. It was the default position of "rest" for any soldier worth his salt as it let him relax while still being ready to engage a threat. The deep quiet of this Iraqi night, though, had let him relax a little more. It had been a constant fight and the far-off echo of machine gun fire—probably another unit of Rangers doing what they do best—was oddly comforting.

Aguirre keyed his mic again from further up, and the "chirp" of the squelch breaking on Byron's radio came in clear in his right ear. "All right boys, take us on through to Cleveland, and then we'll link up at outpost Ferrari."

Byron heard the rest of the guys as they stood, shouldering any gear they had put down during the break and making any adjustments to their own equipment as needed. Even in the quiet of the night, vigilance was a priority. No one was ever relaxed. Not really.

And when the AK gunfire rang out Byron remembered why. Danger close.

"Five o'clock high!" Aguirre shouted. They didn't need to use their radios since the threat was right on them. No time to bother with keying a mic. "Three shooters!"

Byron scrambled to find cover. The road they were on had been lined with apartment buildings, and they mostly kept close to the walls for just such a reason. Ducking into a nearby alley, Byron looked up to find the source of the gunfire and his Nogs lit up with white as bullets exploded from their chambers above. There were at least three gunmen, like Aguirre had said, and none of the men in his squad had seen them. They had no overhead ISR coverage tonight as routes Dallas and Cleveland were both relatively safe—and they were close enough to outpost Ferrari that none of the insurgents would want to be near there.

Unless they were planning something that our intel guys had failed to pick up on.

Aguirre suddenly whirled and took aim at one of the figures firing at them, exhaled slowly, and squeezed. On semi-auto, his rifle was sending out a single shot at a time; lightly, he popped off two more rounds.

"Washington! We got a Humvee on fire up ahead, possible friendlies inside," shouted Aguirre.

He heard shots from behind him, along with Martinez hoarsely shouting "Move! I got you!"

Time to do my thing, Byron thought, and he was off and moving tactically, rifle pointed ahead and looking through the sight.

As he rounded the corner to where Aguirre had pointed, a churning inferno reared its head, washing out his Nogs and forcing him to close his eyes and turn his head. He reached up and flipped up his goggles—they would be useless in the light of the blaze. Blinking a few times, Byron let his eyes adjust to the darkness and looked back to the fire.

In front of him was a familiar tan Humvee. Inside were the silhouettes of two figures. Americans! All around the Humvee were flames. Not good.

He ignored the trap warning from Aguirre. His first and only thought was to help. His medic instincts—his drive to protect—compelled him forward. Still looking through the scope of his rifle, he approached. The sweat on his forehead intensified as his body was suddenly faced with a new source of strain. He quickly swept his gaze over the Humvee, keeping his rifle aimed ahead, and determined the path to be clear. He wasn't sure how long the two figures inside had been there, but the black and white of the infrared American flag patches on their shoulders confirmed their status.

These men needed help.

Slinging his rifle across his back, he raced toward the Humvee. He heard the crackle of comms in his ear but couldn't make the words out. He thought he heard the voice of Martinez behind him as well, but he was too focused on getting to the two men. Then with the next stride, *boom!*

He felt warm, sticky blood cover his face. *Wipe it off, Byron, so you can see!* But his hands wouldn't listen to him. Dimly he saw a teammate race through the smoke to him. He felt himself lifted off the ground.

Then, the world went black.

Byron knew that he was in a C-17 because of how loud it was. As his eyes opened, the scene around him was blurry, but a few blinks brought it back into focus. He saw the IVs that were feeding into his arm—one attached to a bag of blood and the other to a bag of drugs. *I'm on a life flight*, he thought.

"Morning, sunshine," came a familiar voice beside him. Byron saw a figure lean over him, grinning with tobacco-stained teeth. "Took you long enough."

"What happened?" Byron croaked. He barely recognized his own voice. "Where are we?"

"On our way to Wiesbaden, Germany," Martinez answered. "You got real launched back there. You stepped on an IED trying to get those two guys out of the Humvee which, it turns out, was a trap. There's a good clinical team on board, but I wanted to go along for the ride."

Byron winced as he suddenly became aware of sharp pains all throughout his body. He felt his pulse spike and heard a loud beep from the heart monitor.

"Easy, easy," Martinez said in a calm voice. "They got drugs for that. Here," he said as he wrapped Byron's hand around a small button connected the IV. "Press. You're always taking care of all of us. Let me take care of you."

Byron pressed the button, a PCA pump that would send painkillers through the tube in his forearm, and felt a cool sensation wash over him. Before the drowsiness kicked in, though, he heard Martinez lean over and whisper, "Been thinking this could be my last deployment or maybe one more.

"You know anything about my hometown, Pittsburgh?"

SEE WHAT CAN BE

Jeb the fireman and Byron the repaired ministry-medic were outside waiting for me.

Here I am, Sophie Alsas, in Sam-the-Jeep, outside Pittsburgh Firehouse 9. **What am I doing?** *¡Tengo falta un tornillo!*

Byron gave me a crushing hug. I got an awkward side-hug from Jeb.

They swept me inside, and before I knew it, I was in a firehouse. Jeb and Byron took me around to meet everyone and inspect equipment. Jeb's introduction was straightforward: "This is my friend Sophie Alsas. She's a reporter." The whole team assumed I was a new girlfriend, but it couldn't have been the hug. I sat in the fire truck and learned some of the terms. Apparently, a fire 'truck' has a ladder and a fire 'engine' is the one that pumps water. Who knew?

A tall African-American team member, 'Big Mike,' explained the process of firefighting to me. His leathery skin and gray hair gave him a weathered look. He was a firehouse vet and a good teacher. "The first thing we do is 'start the attack,' where we go at the fire to keep it from spreading. Then we 'knock it down' by reducing the flames on the burning edge by cooling it with dirt, water, or other retardants. Finally, we clean up, or 'go into overhaul,' and return things to normal—remove burned material and such. Then Byron here and his paramedic friends patch us up."

I nodded and thanked Big Mike for the explanation. I turned my attention to Byron, who was looking through a bag.

"What's in your duffle?"

I could see immediately that 'duffle' was the wrong word.

"It's a paramedic kit, holds all my gear. With my military medic experience and some classes, I'm a qualified paramedic. I can start an IV, intubate, administer drugs, use a defibrillator, and in general hold off death." He grinned. "I pull duty with Jeb's team once in a while. I still have the guardian angel thing going on in here," he said, tapping his chest.

I stayed until late evening and got a lot of attention from everyone except Jeb. I guess he told his teammates about my dad and my fear of fire. They all worked to show me how they kept each other safe. They were a tight group, like brothers and sisters in a hard-working family. Still, with all of the fires springing up regularly, the firehouse buzzed with suppressed energy.

Byron moderated the tension with a combat-honed calm presence. He spoke with authority about 'high consequence' teamwork and team-based survival. He used personal, detailed stories about how to teach, encourage and build a team.

Hearing all about firefighting and saving the world made me anxious. I played with Dad's Wheaton College ring that I kept on a necklace. I continued my listening. It turned out that the fire station was known for its great work on the job and also out in the community. A core group of firemen focused on discipleship just like The House on campus, making them the 'second discipleship house.' The discipleship reputation drew mixed comments from other firehouses.

Jeb and Byron led me to a small office out of the main flow of the firehouse. It was evident that the two men were tight friends. It was also clear that the two wanted to speak with me together to frame a lot of the elements of my upcoming experience. I got a lot of good framing.

The Applied Servant Leadership work — they called them practices ("because we have to practice to get good at them," Jeb said) — was employed both at The House and the fire station. The practices were the visible expression of the heart for seeing and serving differently with others in community. A community can be The House, a family, the brothers and sisters in a firehouse, or a neighborhood. "It's not just techniques for leading. For us it's doing what is consistent with how we see God and the immense value we see in every person we serve or serve with. With seeing God differently, it's easier to take Him up on His invitation to overcome injustice with good. Seeing others differently makes it easier to see everyone as worthy of our best and our teammates as capable of bringing their best to our work."

I learned that Byron had worked himself back into shape and into a role with the fire department out of a protective concern for Jeb and his teammates in the face of the growing number of dangerous and suspicious fires in the city. "Honestly, the very last thing I wanted to do in my transition to a peaceful civilian life was to hang around firefighters. But Jeb and his buddies aren't going to stop, and I have to be with them to help," he said.

Time for reporter mode.

"Let's take right here at the firehouse. Tell me about your Applied Servant Leader practices that come out of 'see differently.' What does that mean and what does it look like here?" I took a lot of notes and managed to get down a few good quotes to use later. Here's what I got.

Seeing God as always with us and for us invites us to join Him for this time 'behind enemy lines' to overcome evil with good.[5] Sounds like Robin Hood behind the lines, or the Jedi resisting the empire. I see I've joined the resistance.

Jeb gave me some good quotes: "Our joy is protecting and rescuing people. Servant Leaders see people as totally valuable, worthy of respect and never as a means to some end. Byron said, "People *are* the end that God has in mind. We join Him in valuing our teammates and those we serve every day in every way we can, for as long as we can."

"Sorry guys, the buddy-buddy hero story has been done a hundred times. You've got to give me more." I smiled big to show my elusive 'I'm kidding' side. "Say more on Serve Differently."

"Right. Here's one. Take the fire station," Jeb said. "We are the ultimate 'stuck in reactive mode' organization. The alarm goes off and we run. Any leader or team stuck totally in reactive mode rarely does good thinking about being productive. Instead of only being reactive, we try to see what's possible, proactively, to serve."

"How do you get proactive in the reactive firefighting business?"

---

5   Willard, Dallas, *The Divine Conspiracy: Rediscovering Our Hidden Life in God* (San Francisco: Harper), 1977.

Byron answered. "We try to get ahead of the fires. Jeb and his team have been really active in the community to prevent fires." Byron paused and stared at Jeb. He cleared his throat.

Jeb finally picked it up, "We get to know families, landlords, churches, and our local police force. We get invited in to educate on the safety of a home heater, cleaning fireplaces and chimneys, safe cooking. We get a few good meals. We get to the source of a potential fire before it starts."

"Go on," Byron said. "Tell the rest."

"Oh yeah, and we notice when families don't have enough to eat or are cooking on some illegal contraptions because the power is off. We coordinate with churches and ministries to help. We try to serve more than anyone would ask or imagine, do all we can and more because we join God in the work He is already doing."

"How does the reputation for Christian stuff in the firehouse go down with others?"

"It's all good," Jeb shrugged. "We're a high-performing and inclusive team. Anyone who isn't into the Christian worldview is welcome, so there is a list of Christians and non-Christians waiting to get into Station 9. We're just good at what we do."

Big Mike spoke up from behind me, his voice a deep rumble. "We do have serious enemies, Jeb. Some people hope we fail." Then Big Mike dropped another storyline, a big one. "One of the guys downtown on the arson squad told me it looked like someone out there wants to hurt firemen with these arsons. I'm sure he meant us."

Jeb did not look surprised at all. My reporter Spidey-sense started tingling.

Jeb read my mind and took me further. "Sophie, let me show you the hotspots of Pittsburgh." He walked me to a well used, pin-laden map. "These are areas where the suspicious fires have occurred." More than a few of the fires were at churches and community buildings, each of which was designated with a special pin. My investigative brain began to work.

"The fires more or less cluster around our station here in Central Oakland. We're in the college town area of the 'burgh with Pitt, CMU, and Carlow all right here. As you can see, there have been fires at Belltower Church, a Catholic high school, and the Chinese church right around the universities in Oakland. South Oakland is mostly college housing, but we did have a fire at an Orthodox cathedral and at a campus ministry house near there. Then in North Oakland and the Hill District, there were fires at a community center and an AME church. This is a dense urban environment, so having all these fires so close to other buildings and houses is pretty serious."

These were communities I knew. "What about the fires in Squirrel Hill? That's right over near where I live." I asked.

"One is a large historic church in the community and the other is a small church plant that meets in part of an old movie theater."

"Oh, so that's what that is," I said recalling the sign out front of the movie theater. "I've seen tons of kids going in and out of there after school some days."

"Yeah, Young Life runs an after-school program for Allderdice High School students on Wednesdays. I stopped by once, there were tons of kids just hanging out eating pizza and studying after school."

The map in combination with this new information brought questions to my investigative mind. "That's a lot of faith-centric buildings, Jeb. Do you think the arsons have a faith angle to them?" I went further. "Are the fires aimed at you all at Station 9?"

But before Jeb or Mike could answer, a loud wail sounded. I jumped. The loudspeaker called out an address, and the fire team sprung into synchronized action. Byron, already suited up, joined them. I realized I was going to be left behind.

"I'm coming," I insisted, surprised at my own boldness.

Jeb hesitated, then said, "Okay, follow us, but stay out of the way! You won't be able to keep up, so you can just meet us there."

"Be careful!" I shouted. The phrase sounded foolish to me.

Jeb was wrong, I did keep up. Sam scrambled after them through the urban Pittsburgh neighborhoods, whipping around corners and accelerating. In minutes we were at the fire.

It was terrifying.

I stayed in the safe confines of my Jeep, but I could still feel the intense heat and smell of the acrid smoke. I saw the firemen rescue a frail elderly couple from the house just before their car in the garage blew up with an explosive BOOM. The old woman was carrying a giant old book in her arms. Byron and a woman with paramedic bags administered oxygen and care to the couple. Fire totally consumed the house behind the firefighters before collapsing with a sickening crash. It was like a movie set. Dad's final moments in the fire flashed through my head. My eyes followed Jeb through the wreckage. *Sophie, you're at a fire and now in the middle of a fire story. What are you doing?* Did Ben-the-Legend somehow plan for me to get involved with the arson story? Is he that clever?

When the fire was out, Jeb made his way over to me, looking exhausted. He was covered in sweat and reeked of smoke. He was breathing heavily and had to wait, leaning on Sam, until he could talk. I rolled down the window fighting the urge to drive away.

"Everything is OK. They've started the overhaul. I wanted to come over and check in. You OK, Sophie?"

I managed to say 'yes,' but I was lying. Jeb looked at my hands, knuckles white from gripping the steering wheel. I knew if I let go, I wouldn't be able to stop them from trembling. I was nauseated.

"You don't look so good. Do you want to talk about it?"

I slid out of my little Jeep and just said it, all of it. "Jeb, I hate, hate, hate fires. My dad was essentially cremated in a place that still isn't on most maps."

Jeb sighed, shook his head, and put a hand on my arm. "Sophie, I'm so sorry. I didn't mean for this to hurt you."

I closed my eyes and nodded. "I won't quit. Will you help me?"

"Okay. If you're up for it, I can take you deeper. I've got a next step in mind."

"Deal."

I drove Sam home, or maybe Sam drove me home. Of course, there was a power outage on my block when I got there. The street lights and the lights in my apartment building were pitch black. My clothes totally stank of smoke. I threw them away. In darkness, I curled up with Max. Dad, Jeb, and the couple from tonight were a merry-go-round of images. Max whined for an hour with me. I downloaded a fire and police scanner app for my phone so I could start listening for Station 9.

WAY POWER –
BUILDING EFFECTIVE ORGANIZATIONS

Jeb's call was my wake-up alarm. Once he checked in to see if I was OK, he got straight to the point. He came across as a bit curt over the phone, but I guessed he didn't mean it. "I want you to meet some special people, friends of mine. It might help you. You'll have to take the visit 'off the record.' You're going to hear things you will want to write about but you can't. Not yet anyway."

"I agree to take this off the record."

Then he said it, "You're going to meet the Arson Investigation Team. Give me your address and I'll pick you up."

I dressed in a hurry and rushed downstairs. His ride was a candy apple red retro Camaro, a mini fire truck. I was over-the-top nervous.

"Jeb, so sorry I was a mess last night. Question. The woman last night, what was she carrying?"

"People save their most precious possessions in a fire. We see kids and pets. Also photos, books, jewelry, and research. The woman was carrying a family Bible."

I pulled out my necklace. "It's like the ring from my dad's plane."

"I'd like to hear more about him."

A fast drive later we arrived at what I had always assumed was an abandoned brick and stone firehouse on Penn Avenue. We rose in a freight elevator staffed by a policeman and got off on the third floor. The floor was laid out as a high-tech open design workspace. There were high-density screens, photos, marked-up street maps, and lots of bright multi-colored sticky notes everywhere. I read notes on the boards. I tried to memorize: 'DNA,' 'Patterns,' 'Photos,' and more. This was the crime investigation war room for Pittsburgh's Arson Investigation Team and it looked just like something from a TV show. I guessed I was the first reporter allowed in here. Miracle!

Jeb was watching. "Remember, off the record, this is background stuff."

A short, plain looking woman in her sixties split away from the group on the other side of the room and walked briskly over to greet us. She wore a pinstriped suit, short heels, and a gun. "I'm Dorothy Ottey," she said. "Everyone calls me Dot." She scanned me like she was taking in every detail, searching for clues. She said, "Jeb vouched for you. Keep everything you see here to yourself."

Jeb said, "This is Dot's Arson Investigation Team. Dot's an alumnus of The House and a great investigator."

"It's so quiet in here," I said.

"Soundproof," Dot replied, "And electronically secure. We don't want the bad guys knowing what we're talking about."

"Bad guys, in the plural?" Dot frowned, then smiled.

She changed the subject. "Can't go there right now."

"These are smart, dangerous guys we're after and they won't stop. We want to get them and we will. Let me introduce the team. I know you are learning how servant leaders piece together teams.

"This is Tom." He looked like Mr. Rogers to me, down to the half-zipped cardigan and sneakers. "Tom can walk into a room he's only been in once years ago and notice anything that's changed. The slightest angle change of a picture, a notepad in a different place, how the floor has been polished, you name it, he sees it. It's his superpower." She smiled at her own joke.

"I've always had it," Tom said. "When I was a kid, it drove my mom crazy. There's a lot of obsessive compulsiveness that comes with this 'gift.'"

"Tom can walk into a fire scene and see anything that doesn't belong, something an arsonist has left behind, maybe a signature of the arsonists."

I noticed she used a plural again.

"Every arson investigator is trained to look for patterns. I just see them faster," Tom added.

"Tom's the best in the world, you can read one of his forensic investigation books under his pen name when all of this is over. I asked for Tom right away when I put this team together. Tom's been to every fire scene and remembers everything about each one. He compares each scene to others looking for patterns. He's created promising breakthroughs that we're building on right now."

"Breakthroughs?" I repeated, hoping for more.

Dot didn't bite. Instead, she introduced Jerome.

"Call me Jerry," he said.

No last name from Jerry either.

"Jerry, tell Sophie about your role on the team."

"I'm the relationship guy. In a major investigation, we need to coordinate with the FBI, county officials, politicians, forensic units in Washington, civilian forensics, and campuses like Pitt and CMU. We've got close to a dozen partners."

I sucked in my breath. "A dozen agencies?"

"Not all agencies," Jerry corrected.

Dot commented, "This is a major investigation and Jerry knows everyone—the lead people, their kids, where they went to school, what teams they root for, and most importantly he knows how to get the best out of everyone. It's his superpower."

I was meeting the Marvel Comic Avengers.

Lastly, Dot introduced Carl, who was fidgeting and having trouble standing still. "I'm the push, the project manager," he said. "Every day, I help us make progress. My background and love is project management — I like to see key tasks done every day. Right now we're up to eleven interlocking streams of investigative work."

He pointed outside the conference room to eleven very large, moveable boards. "Those are the investigative work streams put together as PERT charts. I keep us organized and on task by keeping track who's accountable for what step and what comes next." The rest of the team nodded in agreement.

Dot had the final word. "Like I said, these are smart, dangerous guys we're after, and we know they won't stop. We want to get them, and we will." She was admitting to me that they were after a team, bent on doing more harm.

As I took it all in, Jeb pointed out the obvious. "This is a well-formed arson team. A servant leader makes a way to succeed by building powerful teams."

Dot nodded. "We complement each other well. Tom notices details, but he can get too caught up in them. Carl can take the details that Tom notices and organize them. It helps to work with a partner. Jerry's able to communicate the resulting organizational direction to partner organizations and gain their coordinated help. I'm the orchestra conductor. A servant leader works to build seamless, syncretistic and effective teams from individuals with complementary knowledge, skills and abilities. We say '1+1=3.'"

A servant leader works to build seamless, syncretistic and effective teams from individuals with complementary knowledge, skills and abilities. We say '1+1=3.'

"How do you build an effective team from a servant leadership perspective?" I asked.

She slid a prepared card over to me. "We establish what we call a 'thinking environment.' These are our practices."

Creating a Thinking Environment

1. **Listen and provide attention.** Look at the person who is talking, let others speak uninterrupted, wait until the person is done speaking before saying anything.

2. **Ask questions to help people reframe limiting assumptions.**
For example, "My opinion doesn't count", to "If you knew that your opinion is vital to our success, how will you address this issue?"

3. **Establish equality** by giving equal turns and attention, and keeping to agreements and boundaries *(time, topics, etc.)*

4. **Appreciate** more than criticize *(Asset-Based Thinking.)*

5. **Stay present,** and free from rush or urgency.

6. **Allow feelings** to be expressed *(don't deny or rescue.)*

7. **Supply accurate information** by providing a full and accurate picture of reality.

8. **Honor differences** *(diversity)* between people.

Adapted from: A Time to Think: Listening to Ignite the Human Mind, Nancy Kline, 1999

When we finished, I was spent. Dot and I ended the day in the conference room alone.

"Jeb told me you lost your Dad in a fire. I lost my sister in an arson twenty years ago." Dot's demeanor softened. "That's why I'm in this job. I'm always looking for that arsonist. I've been where you are. If you want to talk about your Dad, just call me, anytime." Then she read me and spoke something fearful. "I can tell you, off the record, that our arsonists are likely targeting Station 9."

That's where we ended.

At home, I finished up an easy story on new tech businesses opening up in Lawrenceville. I called Mom to give her an update, hinting at the fires and my surprising feelings for a fireman. I left out that I was starting to read a little in my Spanish New Testament that Dad had given me when I was little.

I called Ben next to give him a cryptic update. I told him enough to let him know I was getting pulled into the arson story. The Legend didn't sound surprised.

That was telling.

"Okay, now you have two stories. Finish The House story. Stay connected to the arson story and stay close to your fireman Jeb. He's the key, I suspect."

I had been working the Ben long enough to trust his intuition. So I planned to stay close to Jeb, for the sake of the story. That's what I told myself, anyway. The arson story would have to wait for another day or so. I was headed back to The House tomorrow morning for a training session.

The streets around The House were closed for a street fair. I parked Sam at a distance. I picked up a collection of earrings as I zigzagged through the food, art, candles and fun. I love my city. I spotted a dozen people from my stories on the ethnic communities in the 'Burgh'.

I still managed to get to The House on time. It was packed. Up front was a huge poster.

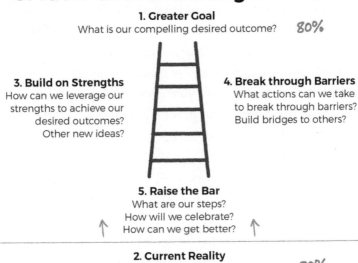

Greater Goal Coaching for Teams

1. Greater Goal
What is our compelling desired outcome? *80%*

3. Build on Strengths
How can we leverage our strengths to achieve our desired outcomes? Other new ideas?

4. Break through Barriers
What actions can we take to break through barriers? Build bridges to others?

5. Raise the Bar
What are our steps? How will we celebrate? How can we get better?

2. Current Reality
Where are we now? What is working? Strengths? Barriers? *20%*

Adapted from: Your Life as Art, 2003, and The Path of Least Resistance, 1984, Robert Fritz

There were more than a hundred participants and a dozen or so organizations in The House. To my utter surprise, Ben-the-Legend and a small team from our newspaper were there. We were to apply a powerful applied servant leadership tool to ourselves and to our team.

"Ben, I'm glad you're here. Thanks for letting me know," I added sarcastically That last part was sarcasm.

"Sorry, Sophie. Join us. You are reporting, and we are working on our own organization. Take off the reporter hat and join the experience with us. This is about making a way for others to succeed."

I was a teammate in running the newspaper.

We started by describing our greater goal, where we aspire to be, and why we wanted to be a newspaper that told the truth, served our readers and communities and was a healthy and caring environment in which to work.

Then we switched to making a way for the team to succeed together. We planned on building on our teammates' assets, knowledge, skills, abilities, goodwill and other capabilities. We also talked about past successes we could draw on to make rapid progress.

We planned for how we could provide needed resources and help for our shared success. Then we made an action plan and committed to each other that we would do our part.

At the end of the experience that morning, every team at The House, including The House staff, had a blueprint to achieve their stretch goals and a template to coach each other daily as a servant leadership team along the way.

After that, Byron spoke to the group. He said, "Now we're going to visit a House alumni. Can we all meet at the Cairo Coffee House in about 45 minutes? Steve Morris, is an alumni who heads the Youth Outreach Center above the coffee house. He will meet us."

I took an Uber. I didn't want to hunt for a parking spot, and Julie had to work. I was the first to arrive. I'm a semi-frequent customer at Cairo Coffee, so the baristas know me. I love good local coffee shops and enjoy blending into the background. I got an Ecuadorian fair trade coffee brewed perfectly.

On the walls were big photos of kids I could have played with back home. The card under the photos explained that the coffee helped children in Ecuador. That added to my guilt. Why don't I go back with Mom on her next trip? I immediately thought I heard in my head: *'come and see.'*

Byron appeared just outside the window, and as usual, he was up to something. He eventually ambled in with a homeless guy who had on a tattered camo military jacket and a battered backpack. Byron bought him coffee and two huge sandwiches. He ate one immediately. I had walked right by the man. I watched Byron's familiar ritual of a close-in prayer, a big hug, and a squeeze on the shoulder. The man was pretty shaky, so Byron helped ease him into a chair in the center of the shop. A few people moved away and maybe, to my shame, I would have too. *Dear God, I want to be different.*

After a while, Byron waved me over and collected a heavyset man with flecks of grey in his hair, Steve Morris. We talked as the rest of the group trickled in around us.

Steve said, "Welcome to the Cairo Coffee House and the Youth Outreach Center upstairs. Bring your coffee — good, right? And let me give you a taste of the ministry upstairs." He led us up a set of wooden stairs lined with dozens of photos of happy kids. Upstairs a spacious room with exposed brick walls and hardwood invited us in. The room was filled with computers, tables, and bookshelves crammed with board games and books. It was clearly a well-loved hang-out place.

Steve explained, "Youth Outreach Center opened five years ago as a part of a community development effort. A group of local social entrepreneurs got together to listen, survey, and assess the deep needs of the community and found that the biggest need was for a safe place where at-risk kids could go after school. A church took the lead to open the Youth Outreach Center and Cairo Coffee House. Their plan was that ongoing funding would come from the coffee house downstairs, and let me say: the plan is working. We're blessed!" Steve held up his cup of coffee and with a "Yay, God," took a sip. I could tell he was struggling to control his emotions. We waited patiently for him.

I opened my notebook. "Can you say more about how you serve students?"

"Yes, I can explain things with the best of them. *Estoy feliz que tú estás aquí Sophie.* I'm glad you're here." He knew me. Steve continued, "Most of the kids in this neighborhood qualify for subsidized school lunches. Sixty percent of the kids come from single-parent homes. For some kids both Mom and Dad are absent. It can be isolating and lonely when your parents aren't around. It's demotivating. Our kids face hunger, rough home environments, and hopelessness. We go right to serving them by providing food, a safe and fun place to hang out, and world-class mentoring. Mentors, including myself, work to give the kids hope that they can succeed in life. We don't just break the barriers — we obliterate them."

A young African-American man picked up the explanation. "You could say our after-school program is really a mentors-and-meals program that focuses on pairing mentors with small groups of students. Kids come in after school, get a large snack, hang out, and play games for a bit. Then around four p.m., kids work on schoolwork and mentors assist them with tutoring and what you'd call life coaching. At six, volunteers feed the kids a full meal before they go home. You'd be surprised at how hungry the kids are. Our aim is to serve these kids practically."

"How do kids find you all?" Someone asked.

Steve answered, "Our referrals come from school guidance counselors, churches, and our own outreach to parents. But really our kids bring other kids. Students bring their friends who bring their friends. This is now a cool place to be."

Byron put his hand on Steve's shoulder. "Why don't you tell the group what made you want to start something like this?"

Steve's voice wobbled a bit. "A youth pastor, this guy Kevin, saw past my crazy behavior and loved me. I had a rough childhood and suffered some abuse, but Kevin saw me differently. He helped me find counseling and provided a safe place for me when I needed it. He was from The House. The original House."

As he finished, a stream of kids flowed into the space from the stairs. They went right to a computer or the bookshelves, paying little attention to us.

We talked for another half hour with Steve about the Mentors and Meals program. We heard stories of kids and mentors who were changed by the program. Afterward, Byron offered to walk back with me toward campus. I knew he would continue teaching.

"In The House ministry, we adapt and overcome. The enemy gives us all kinds of trouble, but we're on to his evil ways." He wagged his index finger in the air.

I was used to his humor.

"We've joined a divine conspiracy to overcome evil with good. We survey our team leaders about what can help them with their work. We serve them to create success."

"For instance?"

"Oh, finding space to meet, getting engaging Bible study materials, providing lots of food to attract students — students are always hungry. Sometimes it's working around policies that more or less try to edge us off campus. That sort of thing. When our team leaders get stuck, we jump in. We make sure they get the Way-Power help they need." He stopped to tie his shoe.

"Byron, you seem so well-adjusted, in fact thriving, in campus life. How do veterans struggle with life after the military?"

"Let's sit." Byron motioned to a bench. "There is some pretty good research on this struggle by the Pew Foundation. Don't think that I haven't struggled with my own adjustment to civilian life. The good news is that returning vets who get involved in a relatively serious faith life have a nearly seventy percent higher increase chance of making what is defined as a good transition. I'm in the middle of a caring ministry. On the other hand, the studies point out that vets with serious injuries or exposure to violent and traumatic events have a more difficult time. I've got the boxes checked on both of those. I'm doing okay and want to focus on helping my other brothers and sisters."

"I'll look at the study. What has been challenging for you in the transition back home, and how have you dealt with it?"

"First, let me offer you another paradigm besides 'coming back home.' I was always at home with my military brothers and sisters overseas. The thing I miss from my military time is the teamwork, the absolute focus on a high purpose mission. What really helps me here at The House is discovering that teamwork again. I'm teamed with my brothers and sisters in Christ in pursuit of the great commission. In an odd way, my time in the military prepared me for this high consequence teamwork."

"Really, Byron? This is just a bit too much."

"I can't help you there. It's my experience. It's my story and I'm sticking to it." He laughed a deep belly laugh.

"Okay, give me another example of what you faced coming out of actual combat. I have no idea."

"For me, it starts with fear. Anyone who tells you they're not afraid in conflict situations is probably shading the truth. We're all afraid, and when I came back home, that fear didn't go away. I thought if I made it through combat, that somehow beating the odds set me up for something bad happening to me back home. I am afraid of being in crowds. I watch for cars getting too close that might blow up, weird things like that. It's hard to explain."

"You live in fear?"

"Other brothers and sisters I served with have it worse. My faith helps me. Jeb has had to deal with this in his work too. We both believe we are 'unceasing spiritual beings with an eternal destiny in God's great universe.' I believe that we're never really going to experience anything like most people describe as death. I imagine it's going to be just like walking through a doorway and spotting some of my friends. I'm especially looking forward to meeting my friend Jesus."

"I wish I had your faith."

"You're doing fine, Sophie. You're asking questions. That leads to good things. We're all here for you. Thanks for spending the day with us. I'm going to head home for the night. Hey, feel free to give me a call if you ever have questions or just want someone to listen to all those thoughts in your head."

FIRETRAP

I didn't sleep well that night. I mean, worse than my normal tossing and turning. I knew for sure now that Jeb's team was being targeted, and it terrified me. I decided to take Byron up on his offer. No sense keeping all these worries in my head. So, I took a deep breath, exhaled, and called my new friend Byron. I told him about my concerns for Jeb and the rest of the team at Station 9.

He was painfully direct. "I've seen it before, the enemy trying to lure in the good guys. The firemen at Station 9 are good guys. They are apparently no closer to finding the bad guys."

Byron was the station's earthbound guardian angel, experienced and courageous. It reassured me that he was aware of the situation and on high alert. I figured I better do my part too, just in case. I kept tabs on Jeb through the fire scanner app I downloaded onto my phone. I told myself the app was for work. But it wasn't, not really.

That very night, I heard Station 9 called into action again. I decided to go. I raced to Sam-the-Jeep, praying out loud this time.

"God, keep Jeb and his team safe," I whispered.

The fire was in an abandoned industrial building in Homewood. I spotted Jeb right away, directing his team. Byron was close by.

It was painful to watch. Thick black smoke billowed out of the building. Instead, I shifted to watching Byron, whose watchful gaze kept him ready to aid the firemen with water, encouragement, and his calm presence. Watching Byron work helped me.

I spotted the tactical commander and moved closer to him to see if I could overhear something. I picked up that the Firehouse 9 team was planning an aggressive attack and heard the order to advance into the building. The commander standing by me counted.

"Okay, ready, 1 - 2 - 3, get it!"

I turned to see Jeb lead his team in through the main entrance, running into the building in two lines. I watched the bright helmets and neon stripes on their coats disappear into the dark building. A clock in my head ticked. Then the worst thing possible happened: the roof and second floor of the building collapsed with a sick, deafening boom.

Debris and smoke formed a thick cloud around the building. Time stopped. I felt numbness come over me. The yells of the firemen outside were oddly muffled in my ears. People seemed to move in slow motion as I stood there looking at the rubble. Anyone inside the building was trapped or dead. I wanted to hope but the likelihood that anyone survived was slim. How could I take another loss?

The noises of men shouting instructions and moving equipment got louder. Big Mike and the rest of Station 9 dove straight into the thick haze to begin clearing away the cement, bricks, and fragments of building that had collapsed. I looked for Byron in the chaos of the fire. He was standing close by. As I frantically scoured for some form of life, a movement around the far corner caught my eye. There were shouts and I was able to make out a neon stripe through the smoke. Then, miraculously, Jeb and all of his teammates emerged from behind the crushed building covered in soot. They were alive!

I nearly collapsed. Jeb and the team made it! The breath I didn't know I had been holding rushed out. Jeb spotted me off to the side and ran over.

"Hey, you OK?" he asked as he got close.

"How'd you guys... survive?"

"We were prepared. Byron suspected the arsonists might be listening to the command radios and planning to pull something. He coached me. When I led the team into the building, I knew instantly something was off. I ran my team right back out the back door just as the second floor came down. We've stayed radio silent in case the bad guys are listening. I'm sure the collapse was remotely triggered. It was engineered to kill us."

Someone yelled for Jeb.

"Hey, I gotta go get back to work. I wanted to let you know that I'm OK." He gave me a hug. I was mostly hugging hot equipment.

SERVE DIFFERENTLY

was a mess. How could I pursue a friendship, let alone a serious relationship, with someone who could be taken from me at any moment? I had to find a way to work on The House story.

The way I understand it, seeing God differently — as they practice at The House — allows them to do what is good for God.[6] At first this struck me as a strange idea, but the more we talked about it, it started to make sense. Luke pointed out to me that seeing what is good for God isn't all that hard, since He told us about it and showed it to us. Generally speaking, it's doing good and great things in service to others. It's building a bulletproof character that allows us to partner with Him. Luke argues that what's good for God is also good for us. That's part of the good news.

And serving people differently means that we start seeing what is also good for them. It doesn't mean that they get their way. A person getting their way can be one of the worst things ever. What is good for a person generally falls in the categories

---

6   Piper, John, "What is Good and Acceptable and Perfect- Thoughts on Romans 12:2." *Desiring God (Blog)*. September 29, 2004. https://www.desiringgod. org/articles/what-is-good-and-acceptable-and-perfect.

of helping them build their capabilities and character, then join others in the pursuit of good and great shared goals.

What is good for a person generally falls in the categories of helping them build their capabilities and character, then join others in the pursuit of good and great shared goals.

I'll admit this is different. A good different, but I just don't know exactly how to describe this yet for my readers.

This weekend was an Applied Servant Leadership teaching time. The House cycled through a public offering on See Differently - Serve Differently every quarter. These experiences were open to students from any campus, nonprofit leaders, government workers, and professionals from the community. House alumni came from out in the work world, some of whom were the teachers for the session.

The coffee at The House, like much American brew, was overdone to me. I went to Common Place to pick up a cup of Costa Rican light roast. The coffee and the cool morning air combined to wake me up.

There was an atmosphere of excitement at The House. Looking around I saw firefighters I recognized standing back near the door. We were in a room crowded with chairs, sofas, and floor pillows organized in large circles. I couldn't find a front of the room to face, but Julie waved me over to where she was sitting on one of the outer rings. I realized that I might be making a friend. Julie handed me a 3x5 card from a stack sitting beside her. Cards were definitely part of their plan to help me learn.

On the top of the card were written the words:

Serve Differently

Julie had told me this session was focused on serving the team to help them achieve their goals. She stood from her spot in the circle to address the crowd. "Welcome to Serve Differently. Our day begins here with some teaching, and then we'll take a field trip with one of our alumni to see how they're putting this practice to work."

We all applauded. Among those clapping was my editor, Ben, with some of my team. He was here! We made eye contact and he laughed at my surprise. That sneak!

Byron wrote on a white board across the room: "A servant leader first sees others on the team differently and empowers them. We then proceed to serve them. Total power grows when it's given away."

A servant leader first sees others on the team differently and empowers them. We then proceed to serve them. Total power grows when it's given away.

Byron opened his Bible: "Jesus said in Mark 10:45 that 'The Son of Man didn't come to be served, but to serve, and to give his life as a ransom for many.'"

Then one at a time, five students rose and read the same thing in different languages, including Spanish. I couldn't help but 'hear' Dad say the words in Spanish. I imagined these words being repeated in a thousand places around the world in every language.

Byron added, "In Matthew 10:1a, 'Jesus called his twelve disciples to him and gave them authority.' Jesus *shared his power* with his first followers. He still accomplishes His work by *empowering* His followers today."

Julie stood and asked, "What are some ways we leaders serve here at The House?"

A hand shot up in front of the room, and a really big guy spoke up. "Hey Julie, I've got an example."

"Thanks, Jaden," Julie said.

"My brother and I are football players. You could say we're team experts. I see the leaders at The House serving in the way we do student-led Bible studies. Instead of staff trying to do it all yourselves, you coach and encourage us students to lead studies. We become the leaders and you, Byron, Jeb, and Luke are the behind-the-scenes coaches. Right?"

He stared at his twin brother, putting him on the spot. The brother stammered, his face slightly red, "Uh...right. The staff here gives us the authority and tools we need to lead. We own it and everyone gets more done as a group. Right?" Several of the students nodded in agreement, encouraging the obviously shy man..

"Right," Jaden smiled.

For the next hour, people shared how their work at The House, in their companies, and in government connected with serving differently.

Ben motioned me over to talk. I was excited to see him, but I had a question.

"Ben, why are you having me research The House if you already know all about it? You're an alumnus!"

"I don't want to write the story myself, and I thought you'd benefit from the experience. I think The House and its practices are fitting with what our readers want—something fresh, uplifting, and substantial. Besides you're familiar with Christian culture. I also believe that Serve Differently will help you." He paused, thinking. "My time at The House deeply shaped the way I run our newsroom. I wanted to offer you the chance to be shaped as well. I see a good bit of myself in you, Sophie, so I want to help you become the best reporter and leader you can be. I wanted you to get started on your own."

"Thanks, Ben. I appreciate you. I forgive you this time for holding back on me."

The room merged back into one group and created a flip chart page with all the information people had discussed. I took down notes on the content and the feel of the gathering. Joy, laughter, and closeness permeated the room. It drew me in. It was irresistible.

Julie checked her pink watch. "Field trip time. Let's go see how this works out in the wild! Our field visit is hosted by the founder of Haven House, an organization that serves women who are breaking free from being exploited and trafficked in the sex industry. We won't be able to go to the actual safe house because that location is secret, but the mayor has agreed to host us downtown." There was applause for the mayor, standing in the back with the firemen. I was not surprised to see him here. The mayor's work at this kind of training would raise the interest of my readers.

Julie asked if she and Byron could ride over with me in Sam-the-Jeep. We put the top down to catch the sun. As we drove, I decided to ask Julie about how Serve Differently plays out in a hospital setting.

Julie laughed, "Health care isn't exactly famous for serving your teammates. Many times you have to 'be in charge' in high-consequence circumstances. But high consequences and 'do it yourself' don't go together. What you'd see in our very best units at the hospital are professionals who build and make a way for teams to succeed. Leaders in the best places work to make sure the best ideas surface and get applied. I've worked for some very independent clinicians along the way who have to have the last word. I've seen how that can work against delivering great care. For myself, I love to have my clinical students deliberate and debate right along with me. I get the best ideas that way and I try to give credit where it's due. *It's not about fighting for positions, it's about using your position to empower your team.*"

It's not about fighting for positions, it's about using your position to empower your team.

From the back Byron, pointed out with evident pride in his friend: "You know, Julie winds up with great teams around her, both at work and on campus. She's a good leader and a good doc." I watched him in my rear-view mirror. He patted his leg and the two shared a secret smile. Noted, again.

We pulled up to the large granite and steel city office, parked Sam, and made our way inside. Once through security, we met in a large conference room on the fifth floor. The windows overlooked the busy urban street below. As the group filtered in, the mayor went to the podium at the front of the room flanked by the city, state, and national flags. A woman in her early forties with curly sun-streaked hair joined him. The mayor introduced her as our host, Joan Pierson. As I looked at Joan, I could see dramatic irregular scars on her face and neck. She did not try to cover them.

"Peace to you all and welcome. I'm the director of the Haven House. We provide a safe place for women in extreme danger." Her relaxed manner and chunky wooden jewelry gave off a hippie vibe.

The words "safe place" and "danger" lingered for me.

"Haven House is a ministry for trafficked and exploited women. Many are imprisoned in the industries of pornography, prostitution, and gentlemen's clubs. We make a home for these women. We offer programs to help residents to recover from addiction, to grow spiritually, and master the skills they need for life and employment."

Here's your chance, Sophie. In college I volunteered to help women, but I never stuck with it. Joan looked right at me. "If any of you want to help, we could use volunteers."

She went on. "Let me tell you how God led me here. It's not PG-rated. As a teenager, I got into drugs with my friends. It started as fun, then I was hooked. I was unable to keep up my grades, lost interest in school, and dropped out. My parents weren't much help. I needed money to support my addiction. I became a prostitute."

We were silent.

"It was dark. I didn't have options. I was a hooker hooked on drugs. But God intervened. Women from an East End church here showed up. They didn't judge. A lot of lunches and conversations later, I agreed to try recovery. Those women saved my life." Joan tilted her chin up, wiping back a tear and exposing more scars on her neck. They looked like rope marks to me.

"In recovery, I discovered Jesus. I did my part. With His help and my support group, I made choices for a new direction in life. I got clean, finished a GED program, and went to college at Pitt. I ended up at The House."

There were a few 'yeahs' and claps. We were on her side. I was on her side!

"The House gave me more life. I experienced community, unconditional love, plus great food! I gained thirty pounds, and I needed it. All of the judgment-free support and relentless love I received from Julie, Byron, and the others changed my life for good. I wanted to pay it forward, so I came up with Haven House. I went back downtown to reach women just like me. I had someone I wanted them to meet, my friend Jesus." Joan's smile crinkled up. "Me and Jesus wanted a home where they could be safe."

Come home, Sophie, I heard in my own thoughts. It wasn't me, though.

Julie stepped in with a hug, "Thanks, Joan. Tell us more about how Servant Leadership works here." Julie nodded at me to listen.

There was a little shuffling up front, and Joan was joined at the podium by two other women. We were introduced to Mia and Claire. Mia was one of the shift leaders and Claire was the program director at the Haven House.

Mia spoke first. Her raspy voice reflected years of smoking. "Our job as a leadership team is to make a way for other women in the house to reach the full potential God has for them. Here, the students become the teachers."

I got chills.

Mia continued, her smile broadening. "We lead community living, help with job training, and share our stories. We make a way for the women as servants to them. Questions?"

I asked for examples of day-to-day routine.

Claire answered, "We know that one of the keys is to be fully present — something our residents have a hard time doing. There's no phones or TV during this part of the day. We actually practice just listening to each other, eyes on eyes, no interrupting. And we teach the skills of ordinary life: checkbooks, how to find friends, healthy habits, and accountability. We get close and show love to each other. From the start of the program, the women have to be willing to accept help and be open to learning. This doesn't come easily for women who have always been on their guard for survival. Attending church, participating in a group Bible study, and submitting to monthly drug tests are all essential for staying in the program."

"It's all about love," Mia chimed in. "We learn and teach hope, realistic optimism, and confidence here. We have a daily chores chart at the Haven House that's similar to the one at The House on campus. Women each take turns cooking, washing dishes, cleaning, and picking up in the common rooms. Once they complete their daily chores, they put their initials on the chart — and often an encouraging or thankful message to others."

"Well said, Mia," Claire said with a smile. "Hope and confidence are so important, especially since no real house community would be complete without its challenges. The women are frequently irritated or confused by the other residents. We coach them to effectively address these concerns. Those are skills they can use in their future home and work lives. All of our many volunteers are skilled at teaching how to coach."

With that, from the back of the room, twenty or more women volunteers came up front to join the leaders. Cookies and lemonade magically appeared. We broke into discussion groups to learn from ministry leaders and volunteers.

I particularly connected with Mia. She said everyone was welcome. It didn't matter what anyone had done: after she had left, she was welcome back.

She paused and looked at me. "I first joined the Haven House eight years ago as a client. As much as I liked the community, I missed the comfort of drugs and ended up going back to my old life. Joan and Claire came to find me many times, bringing me stuff I needed. They showed me I was loved even when I made poor choices. I finally asked if I could come back. They all welcomed me with open arms. I've worked hard to stay clean since then. I got a job, and then in just the past year I came back to the Haven House as the shift leader. I'm now a leader and I have so much I want to give back. These women were Christ to me. They took me in even after I walked away."

I found Joan Pearson next and waited patiently until she saw me.

"I'm Sophie Alsas."

"I know who you are, Sophie. How can I help?"

"Could I volunteer at the Haven House sometime?"

"You're more than welcome to volunteer with us, Sophie. Come and see me."

THE CHEFS

The next morning, I checked out my mostly empty shelves. All I had was a leftover meatball sandwich, a few crackers, dog food, and a half-empty box of pasta. "It's time to shop, Max." Max barked and wiggled. He knew that word. I grabbed my purse, pulled on sandals, and headed out to the co-op near Construction Junction.

I was in the middle of the all-natural produce aisle at the store when I thought I saw Jeb in the next aisle. Luckily, I had French-braided my hair and at least changed my t-shirt.

He spotted me too and waved me over. "Hey, Sophie, I promise I'm not stalking you," he joked.

Jeb was in fireman's pants and a navy t-shirt with Station 9 on the front. He was with Big Mike, who towered over him. Both guys had fresh, large bandages on their hands.

"Hi again Sophie, remember me? I'm Mike, we met at the firehouse the other week. Before all the excitement. Last night was busy too." From his back pocket, a radio squawked.

"Of course I remember you, Big Mike! You did a great job explaining firefighting 101."

Jeb said, "We're going on duty. Big Mike and I are making Pittsburgh-style pizzas for the guys tonight: extra meat and extra fries on top."

"You guys can cook?"

"Sure," Big Mike replied, his deep voice filling the aisle. "We make fine pizzas, anyway."

"Cooking isn't my favorite thing, it's not exactly a strength," Jeb said. "But we all take turns cooking, and tonight Big Mike is my sous-chef."

Big Mike corrected Jeb: "It's the other way around. Jeb's *my* sous-chef. It's my years of experience. I also watch cooking channels."

"I wondered what you all do when you aren't out saving the world."

"We stay productive, but we're saving the world a lot these days. What are you up to today?" Jeb asked.

"I'm just getting groceries for me and my guy Max."

A crease appeared between Jeb's eyes. "Max?"

"Max is my dog."

Big Mike, who also saw the reaction, laughed.

"He's my golden retriever. I've had him since he was a puppy. My therapist recommended a dog. They love you and never leave you." *Sophie, what were you thinking?* "Uh, sorry, I shared way too much. I promise I'm not super weird."

Jeb laughed, now smiling. "Good for you and good for Max. I'm glad it's working out."

Big Mike's radio interrupted us with an urgent-sounding call. Mike and Jeb listened intently, leaning on the tomato sauce shelves.

Big Mike said, "Hey man, we should get to the station. Good to see you, Sophie. You're welcome to come by the station for pizza later."

I smiled. "Great to see you too. I still have some work I need to do, so I'll have to pass on the pizza. Maybe next time."

And then they were gone.

Seeing Jeb and Mike in the store got me going. Why not do a bit of independent arson investigation? I could drive by the fire scenes around town. Maybe seeing these places would help me deepen my story. After putting away groceries, I started thinking.

It was time to put my investigative brain to work and use my connections within the community. I couldn't just stay on The House story, all squeaky clean and good. The arsons were now starting to close in on my friends, and frankly, it was making me mad.

I plotted a map through the neighborhoods that had suspicious fires. I called ahead to community leaders and good sources that I knew. I loaded myself into Sam-the-Jeep and made a day of it. Everyone was eager to talk.

Nobody really knew anything, but no one was short on opinions. The bad guys were clearly targeting not only religiously affiliated organizations, but also a community center and, most worrisome, a couple of after-school programs. Both of those had loose religious affiliations.

My last interview was on a porch with one of my favorite community characters. Emma Johnson knew everybody and pretty much everything worth knowing in her community. Her neighborhood had two suspicious fires.

She said, "Honey, you should be careful asking questions like this. I think these are bad people you're asking about. They just might not take kindly to you more or less joining the hunt to find them. I say leave it to the professionals. I'm not going to say you were here, but somebody surely will, and word gets around." She gave me a hug that lingered.

Buildings had been destroyed, but the communities were still strong. Homes opened up for dislodged people and programs. Resilience and resistance were the themes that I kept hearing. But resistance to what? The arsonists were not winning. Pittsburghers are tough.

One of my sources talked about the arsonists. One was a "short muscular man with a black baseball cap" who wore "dark military-style clothing and a slim backpack." A second man was younger, maybe late teens or early twenties, in a dark hoodie. Could be any of a thousand people in the area. I guessed the Arson Investigation Team had all of this.

When I finished, I called Dot. She confirmed my information but warned me, "Sophie, don't investigate in the field alone. These are very dangerous men. Let us find them."

That night I put on a movie and again turned on the scanner. There was a fire call with Jeb's Station 9 responding. I stared at the phone and prayed, this time more sincerely. Me, praying. Max whined. He could tell when I was anxious.

Byron texted me from the scene, as if he somehow knew that I was listening, that Jeb and his team got this fire under control quickly. I was now sure my interest in Jeb was clear to Byron.

I slept fitfully.

I dreamed I was in South America scared about something I saw outside. I saw Dad land our airplane beyond the house. I started running to the landing field, but I couldn't get any closer, no matter how much I ran. I woke up with my legs thrashing off the sheets.

FRIENDS

After a restless night of wandering around the apartment, I was exhausted. I still had to do interval training for my supposed sprint triathlon. I was still unsure about signing up. The running could help me in lots of ways. I laced up my neon orange shoes and decided to run Schenley—the long urban park near campus. The park was a mix of tough hills with trails through green spaces and a public golf course. No music today; just soul-searching.

Pittsburgh's black, glass, and steel downtown was visible above the rolling fog in the distance from the top of the Schenley Oval. I pulled my hair into a ponytail, slipped on a headband to keep any fly-aways in place, and got running. Relaxed upper body, compact stride, head straight. I felt good enough to push it. I had followers, so I put on the afterburner, pulling away from two young guys who had been keeping up with me on the path. They tried to rally, but I slowly pulled away. And this wasn't my top gear.

I started running as a girl in the high altitude of the Andes. I ran all the time and I was fast. Running came easily to me at Miami University, where I discovered that I could run competitively. I walked on and actually made the Miami track team. It was a good sport for me. It was just me and the track most of the time. I ran distance and won a lot. I wish Dad could have seen me.

In the Andes, my parents would let me run by myself to my friend Pilar's home. It was a good distance away. Pilar was a runner too, so we ran everywhere together in the clean thin air. My altitude training gave me a running superpower when I first returned to the States. Cesar and Alba were my surrogate Ecuadorian parents. They routinely kept me overnight and helped me become fluent in Spanish. They taught me the Ecuadorian ways of personal and unapologetic faith in Jesus. Back then, I knew what love and faith felt like. Now I mostly feel empty. I also learned from Alba about beauty. As a kid, I was already known for my looks. Alba explained to me how to be beautiful inside. I'm not sure I'm beautiful on the inside. I've done ugly things.

I had dropped my pace. The young guys were gaining on me. They were in for a surprise. I still had a lot left in the tank, so I upped my pace. We sparred. They were good, but I was better.

In my cooldown, I started reasoning. That triathlon? Ugh! Racing those guys was fun. Swimming just doesn't do it for me. I'm going to save the triathlon for another year and just run. *Focus.*

When I got close to my apartment, I had that weird sensation that I was being watched. I couldn't spot anyone. Inside my building, I forced myself to take the stairs. I unlocked the door and bolt with keys hanging around my neck next to Dad's college ring. I had just showered when my cell phone played my ringtone, the theme from *Friends*— "I'll Be There for You." It was one of the few shows I watched when we came back to the States.

It was Jeb!

"Some of us are going out for dinner—Byron, Luke, Julie, and me. Want to come? You can bring a friend if you want. It's a community practice to eat together." Jeb offered to pick me up.

I texted Darcy. I needed the Darcy buffer. She agreed to meet us there. Wingman!

I spent the day working on a short unrelated story. I still needed to do routine stuff. But I was able to spend time organizing my notes on See and Serve Differently. Mom stopped by to take Max to the dog park. She doted on Max as if he were a grandchild. I enjoyed having her in my place, just being a mom. As she walked around I knew she was praying for me. I let her convince me that she should take Max overnight. But that left me alone.

As darkness crept down, I got a little scared without Max. I called Jeb.

"Want to come over early?"

Minutes later, I watched Jeb get out of his red Camaro—lean, angular, and athletic. I already felt better. He dropped to the pavement and cranked out twenty-one pushups. It was an odd number and he looked good doing them. I opened my door and stared at the elevator. He popped out of the stairwell thirty seconds later.

"Stairs?"

"Always! I'm a lean, mean, fire-fighting machine. Your stairs are nothin'."

Two women I knew were slowing down to get a closer look. Jeb gave them a charming smile and said hello.

I intervened, quickly inviting him inside. "Want a drink? I've got lemonade."

"Yeah, lemonade sounds wonderful." I watched as he sipped, then gulped. "Terrific," Jeb declared. "You could bring gallons of this by the firehouse."

"I take pride in my lemonade. I'm also a pretty good cook—I can make North African dishes, Ethiopian, and some Ecuadorian fare. Well, I mean, my mom likes it … and Darcy … and other people too."

Time for the real talk.

"Jeb, can I bring up … something personal?"

"Yep," Jeb said. But his face said, "nope."

I stalled, then chickened out and didn't ask what was really on my mind. Instead I asked, "Tell me more about yourself, background and such?"

"On the record?" He relaxed both of us with his electric grin. "It's all normal stuff. I practically lived at our church in the southern mountains of West Virginia. My mom was the secretary at the church, so we kids were there all the time playing in the Sunday school rooms while she worked. My dad was the town mechanic, so he's the one who helped me restore the Camaro. We got it cheap, but it needed a year of work to get it where it's at today. Our family had some land since both of my grandfathers were coal miners and hobby farmers. Faith was a constant part of our family. My brother was the one who taught me to pray and read the Bible. He used to practice his preaching on me. He's a minister now. As teenagers we did Young Life together and spent a lot of time with our youth leaders. After high school, I wanted to expand my small-town life, so I came here. I have an older sister, Lilly, who also came up here for school and stayed. She's a critical care nurse at Children's Hospital. She loves kids. I love kids too. I just don't know many."

I gave him more lemonade. He was comfortably silent for awhile, then started again.

"I enrolled at Pitt and then went through some dark stuff. Leaving home was hard. I drank and partied way too much. After one particularly rough night, I decided to make a change. I called my brother. He and some others helped me. The short story is I stopped drinking, dropped out of Pitt, got firefighting training, and joined the fire department. Turns out it was a great choice. I'm good at it. The firehouse I joined, as you know, is *different*. There was a ministry right there, and I was surrounded by committed Christians. I got re-connected with Byron and Luke, who helped me bring The House leadership principles to the firehouse. Serving Leadership is in our work and life culture now."

He paused again and just waited for me to speak. I hesitated, then said, "You know, I'm not exactly the believer I once was as a kid. I know you know that. Can we still be friends? Maybe good friends?" I didn't ask him about a more serious relationship.

Jeb took a good swig of his lemonade. He knew what I was asking. "We're friends, Sophie, let's keep at it. Sure." He looked at his phone, "Speaking of friends, looks like people are headed over. Let's go have some fun."

Well, official friends was a start.

A short while later, Darcy, myself, and 'The House Gang' were all situated at Casbah. Apparently, a donor regularly dropped off gift cards at The House for this top-end restaurant, so all of the staff knew The Gang.

Byron helped us order. An ex-Army friend was the chef and sent out special dishes.

While Jeb and Julie were explaining the basics of The House to Darcy, I reverted to reporter mode. I wanted to dig further into Byron. He was too perfect. "Okay, Byron, you have everything together. Do you even have any gaping weaknesses? Maybe a secret criminal enterprise?"

Byron smiled and nodded, "I've got flat spots. Go easy on me, okay?"

"Of course."

"I can come across way too strong. I'm getting better, but I too often have to 'win' the conversation. I want everyone to meet Jesus. Sometimes I don't listen. I just want them to finish talking so that I can make a point. And let me tell you: it doesn't work."

"What's another one?"

"The chip on my shoulder. My warrior nature comes out once in a while, especially when I feel disrespected. I get angry and definitely nowhere close to 'love your enemies.' It's an inner wound I carry from the racism I've experienced. When I feel disrespected, anger rises up in me. Sometimes I let it show."

"Wow, I'm glad I've never triggered that."

"Yeah, I'm more peaceful now. I don't know how Jesus did it."

The conversation moved on to other things. Two glasses of wine in, I spoke about Ecuador, my years at college, my disappointing life in the 'Burgh, and my dad. I told my story.

"The night before my dad died, we got into a huge fight. I was mad that my soccer coach benched me for goofing off at practice. Dad agreed with my coach. I sulked and stayed home. Dad died the next day."

Nobody spoke. Even the tables around us were strangely quiet. "After he died, we stayed in Ecuador for three years before we moved back to our mission's headquarters here in Pittsburgh. Coming back to the states for high school was hard — it might as well have been a different planet. I never fit in. The pain of losing Dad, in addition to culture shock, left me angry and depressed. I hated my mom for taking me away from my friends in Ecuador and hated God for taking away my father. He's gone. He doesn't even know that I turned out to be so much like him. I used to be able to remember everything he ever said to me, but it's all fading, and I can't get it back."

Byron and Jeb both edged closer to me, moving their chairs. "I mean, how could God take my dad from us just when I needed him the most? He was only doing good things. I don't understand how Dad thought that taking those risks was the right thing for us." I thought that would push back Byron and Jeb.

Instead, Byron moved even closer. "I haven't lost my dad, but I've seen terrible things. Terrible, bad things happen to good people every day. All I know is that we're in a fallen world. I'm so sorry for your hurt, Sophie. I've thought more than a little bit about risk and sacrifice. I bet your dad did too. I also bet we both go back to our role model. Jesus came to show us what God was ready to sacrifice for us. He came to die for us. He not only knew the risks, he was certain of them."

"I don't get it."

Byron got within whisper range. "Could I pray for you?"

I started to say no, but it was too late. Byron put his hand on my arm and prayed right at the table. No one stared.

"God, Father, you love Sophie. She wants to trust you, help her to trust again. You can do things that we can't. Thank you, Amen."

"I didn't say I want to trust Him."

Byron just said, "Come and see me early tomorrow. We'll go for a walk."

TATTOOS ON THE HEART

In the morning, I went to The House. Byron was wearing a Captain America shirt, long-sleeved despite the heat. He guided me to The Table strewn with papers and cleared a space.

Byron said, "More than once downrange in combat, I got into serious trouble. My guys were always there. It worked out. God is *with* me now in everything I do, and He works everything out for good!"

"Okay, Byron. I get it." I'm sure I scowled.

Byron was unruffled. "Sophie, I've got something to show you before we go walk." He opened a portable plastic file and drew out stacks of photos. He arrayed students, firefighters, staff at barbecues, dance parties, bonfires, and meals on The Table. There were pictures of alumni around the world. This was something special to Byron.

"The thing about the kingdom is, Sophie, it's available to all of us. That door is open to outsiders, uncool and unlovely people, addicts, those who are confused, people who are busted up, the weak, the powerless, and every other outsider you can think of. Everyone is welcome. That's the deal. God is for us all."

He looked at his watch. "Let's go walk around and meet some students. Give me a minute and we can go." He disappeared into the kitchen. I followed him part way. He reached high into a cabinet and grabbed a big bottle of white pills. With an experienced twist to the cap, he took one, then a second. "That should help. I'll be good." He steadied himself on the counter. "I think I'm good... I think I'm good."

Just then, Luke walked in from another direction. "Hey man, how are you doing?"

Byron looked up at Luke and said, "I'm good."

"You don't look so good," Luke countered, moving in closer. "Pain?"

Byron spied me in the doorway. "Yes, it's Sophie." He gave me a smile and a wink.

Byron pushed off of the kitchen counter. "Okay, let's go, Sophie." We stepped outside to the busy campus.

"Our staff and the student leaders have hundreds of student encounters each month, most of which are unpredictable and informal. Sometimes it's a problem with a boyfriend or girlfriend, other times they just want to hang out and see what Christian community is like. A surprising number of them grew up without support in life from Mom or Dad."

"I can relate."

"I'm sorry, Sophie. I know that's tough."

"More than tough. He died a hero, so how can I be mad at him? But I am. He wasn't around for anything! He didn't come to my school events, he couldn't take me to college or come to Family Weekend. He didn't give me advice about boyfriends, and he wasn't around to protect me from the terrible, awful stuff that came my way. I was on my own! But I feel guilty for being mad at him."

Byron didn't say anything. He stopped and just looked at me. Then he hugged me.

We wove our way through the mosaic of a modern American campus. I was reminded of myself in this scene at Miami University. Our forward progress was interrupted about every two minutes by students. They stopped Byron to catch up or give him a hug. Students loved him. Byron prayed with most and moved on only when the other person was ready. Guided by radar, he managed to find the veterans in the sea of students. The vets were even more open about their faith — maybe service does that?

We swung through the packed main coffee shop where more students greeted Byron. They didn't have my kind of coffee, so I skipped the java. Byron got two cups of coffee to go. We headed directly to the corner of the quad to what seemed like a prearranged meeting. The extra coffee was for a student vet in a high-tech wheelchair. He was waiting for us. I could tell he was a vet by the camo flag on his hat. Byron held a cup patiently for the young man to drink. Neither of them seemed to mind. In a turn-around, he prayed for Byron. I gave them space.

Byron explained to me later, "He's recovering, and it's a long road. His hands are too wobbly to hold a cup, but because we're brothers, he lets me help him. I'll always owe him." I knew there was more he could say.

I needed a timeout. I retreated to a restroom. When I finally found Byron again, he was with another student.

"Byron, wanna hear my verse of the week?" In the middle of the quad, the student recited scripture word for word perfectly. The verse came to me in Spanish: "All things work together for good…"

We moved on.

"You could do this all day, couldn't you?"

"You bet!"

Byron was in pain. I asked him about it.

"No one hopes for pain, but it comes to all of us. Pain is my constant friend now. Some days are worse than others. Pain helps me depend on Him."

"Okay, that's the Christian thing to say. How are you *really* doing?"

Byron paused and sighed, "The truth is, I've used too much of my painkiller lately. I know the line and I've gone past it." Byron's gaze drifted away as if remembering something he wasn't ready to share. "Don't worry, I'm going to wake up in the morning. Julie's helping. She's working to remove the source of the physical pain. I'm going to see her and have a little procedure to get that last bullet removed."

The shocked look on my face must have been just the reaction he wanted. "Just kidding, not a bullet, probably some of the fragments that got blown into me working their way to freedom. We're going to have to help the little fellows out in the next few days."

He seemed to be considering his discomfort. "C.S. Lewis said that pain is God's megaphone. I've learned things from my hurt, but today I've had enough. Let's head back to The House. It's our International Welcome. It's a 'drop in' kind of thing that stretches on all day and into the evening. There will be food and international Christians like you."

"Like me?" It was sort of true.

Outside The House, clumps of students were talking and laughing. It was the United Nations, only more cool. I don't know how he did it through his pain, but Byron stationed himself by the door and greeted every student. Julie was by his side handing out candles. They were a team. I knew there was more.

Food was prepared to rhythmic music. There were students from Africa, Indonesia, Central and South America, the Caribbean, the Middle East, West Asia, Europe and, well, from almost everywhere. Julie sat next to me and gave me the scoop: "There are hundreds of international students on campus. We reach out to them through dinners, Bible studies, and English practice. We know most are going to go back to their countries to work in God's great kingdom. We want them to be prepared as disciples and leaders. Some of them will go back to serve in places where it is quite dangerous to be a believer. When I go back to Asia, I hope Byron will come and visit me once in a while."

Byron looked at her, then said something I will always remember: "With my whole heart I will go anywhere, anytime that God calls me. I've already settled with Him my willingness to support my sisters and brothers even if it means my life." He said it so directly it stunned me. I just studied my plate.

Jeb Phelps slipped into the group. Though there were plenty of places to sit, he chose a seat across from me, and my stomach fluttered. I watched him in action, encouraging everyone sitting with us, including me.

"So Superman, how's saving the world going today?" I said.

"Well, today we mostly spent time working out to stay in shape and working on our gear. The only excitement was a car fire."

"Okay, that counts." I stood up straight and made my voice go as low as possible, trying to imitate Jeb. "Your car is toast. But how else can I help you, ma'am?"

Jeb laughed, "Good impression. I'm no Superman. Can we walk?"

We found a quiet spot.

"Since we are official friends, you have the right to know a little more. I heard Byron talked with you about some of his challenges. You know about my drinking. It was actually a problem on multiple levels. Drinking led to fighting and a few nights in jail."

"OK... ?"

"That's where I met a good policeman. He steered me toward the fire department. My older brother helped me a lot. In my drinking days, I had a girlfriend. We drank a lot together. When I stopped drinking, I was a lot less fun. It didn't end well. I think she's still in town."

"Not in contact?" I regretted my question.

"Not with her or the others. During my drinking time, there were a number of women. I never let them run into each other, and I thought I could manage them. I couldn't. Eventually, my main girlfriend at the time found out, which contributed to the breakup. Trust me, those days are over. That's pretty much it. I just wanted to make sure you knew I'm no Clark Kent."

"We have a lot in common," I said. "I've done some stuff I'm not proud of. But I don't think I can do the confession thing like you."

"I understand, Sophie. It's not something I usually share."

"No worries."

When the last of the students left, I followed Jeb and Byron into the kitchen. The dishwasher was already full, so we set to work on the remaining pile of the dishes. I squeezed in the middle, dried what Byron washed and handed dishes to Jeb to put away. Up close, with his long Captain America sleeves rolled up and hands immersed in dishwater, I could see Byron's arms covered in tattoos. They were not the usual skin art, just names in black with dates in blood red. They started at the wrist, extending past the elbows to who knows where.

"Byron, I'm probably the last person in The House to know, but these names? Are they soldier teammates you saved?"

Byron stiffened and sighed. He gave me a sideways gracious smile. *Uh oh.* Jeb stepped over to Byron.

"Those aren't people Byron saved."

The truth flooded me. The names were teammates *lost*. He had etched each one onto his body. We continued working in silence.

When I finally stepped out of the kitchen, I looked back to see the two guys leaning on each other.

A GIRL NEEDS HER MOM

had to see Mom. I called and tempted *mi madre* with a girls day out.

Our first stop was the spa. As I drove to the salon, I noticed a battered black car maybe following me. I should have gotten a plate number.

At the salon in Shadyside, Mom gave me her usual mom-hug. Not for the first time, I noticed she was shrinking; my arms wrapped around her shoulders. I still thought of her as in her late thirties, like she was when Dad died. I kept her frozen in time.

While getting our nails done, I watched Mom. She talked so easily, offering love and wisdom to the ladies. She was kind and present. She fussed over me, too. Our nails freshly painted — mine a taupe and Mom's a pale grey — we headed to the second part of our day, high tea at the Frick Cafe in Point Breeze. It's part of Henry Clay Frick's original mansion and grounds. It's fancy.

High tea was something that Dad's mom started with my mom as mother and daughter-in-law bonding. The women in my family have kept up the tradition. Mom knew I needed to talk, so here we were.

The cool morning had melted into an intermittently sunny day. We sat outside one last time before the patio closed for the winter. The warm sun was rare this late in the year. We ordered pots of tea, Earl Grey for mom and chocolate mint for me. The high tea goodies were served on three-tiered trays with sandwiches and quiches on the bottom, scones and fruit in the middle, and cakes, pastries, and chocolates at the top. I brought my own extra blueberries to put on top because I'm obsessive. I needed the fruit on my pastries to be an odd number.

Mom was content to eat slowly, savoring every bite, while I was trying my best to not inhale my sandwiches. Meals growing up had a lopsided rhythm to them. Our shared meals would start quietly with Mom talking and asking questions, while Dad and I scarfed down our food. Once we had finished eating, Dad and I would dominate the conversation debating something as we waited for Mom to finish. She would join in between bites. Mom could take an hour to eat. Dad and I always finished in a flash. I asked Mom about her classes.

"I've been teaching business writing this semester in addition to Intro to Journalism and Nonfiction for freshmen. Juniors and seniors outside the English department take my business writing class to help get a job. Students start off engaged. I find that as the semester progresses, many start skipping class to interview for jobs."

"That bother you?"

"*Me da igual*. I want them to succeed. I'm just happy when they do come. I'm looking forward to getting everyone's portfolios in and graded, and working on my book. My forever book project."

Mid-way through my third finger sandwich (Mom's first), I brought up Jeb. She already knew what was on my mind.

"Let me guess, you think you're falling for an unattainable guy who runs into harm's way and may never come back. And you're afraid you will self-destruct the relationship in some sort of self-fulfilling prophecy?"

"Yep, that's it in a nutshell. I mean, I saw him barely escape death once, but he might die the next time. I wonder where this is really going with Jeb. I mean, could this even work? What if it could work, but I mess it up? *¿Qué debería hacer?*"

"I know, *mi amor*, it's hard trusting God."

"How's this about God?" I said louder than is polite at the Frick.

"It's related. As hard as it was losing your father, I do not regret his sacrifice. My life with him was a great joy. He'd often say, 'Right risks are better than a wasted life.' I agree."

"*Entonces*, I should just be okay with what Jeb does?"

At this point, our waiter looked in our direction, slightly alarmed.

"*Pues*, losing Dad was awful for you. I questioned God, but I let God hold me and heal me. That was our difference."

"I guess." I slopped some clotted cream on a currant scone.

"Have you talked with Jeb about all this, explicitly?"

"*Más o menos*. I don't know, I guess not really. He's a 'committed Christian.' I'm the prodigal daughter. He actually believes that he's called to his work. Where have I heard that before?" I figured that would hurt, but I was on a roll. "Anyway, I'm not good enough for him. What would Dad say about me now? You know: wandering, still alone, stubborn?"

She smiled. "He'd say that you'd never stay somewhere you didn't want to be and that there is nowhere you can go that God won't be there with you. He's waiting for the slightest step back in His direction."

I sat in silence, ironically watching a father and his toddler playing outside of the cafe. The little girl was pushing limits —

climbing everything, and then jumping off. Her father let her go but stayed close.

Mom left me alone to think.

"Mom, I used to pray for Dad every night. That night after our fight I was so mad I didn't pray for him." I paused. "Do you think it's my fault? If I'd prayed would he have lived?"

There. It was out. The damning self-condemnation I've held onto for all this time.

Mom's eyes instantly filled up, "Oh, Sophie. No, no, no!" Reaching out she held my hand tightly. "Your dad was in the center of God's plan even in that fire. I'm glad you're here with me."

She smiled exactly the way Dad used to smile. We sat holding hands, oblivious to the diners openly staring at us.

* * *

At home, Darcy was on a work trip so that night I was alone, except for Max.

Around midnight, Max let me know there was someone at the door. He usually barks, but this time he just went silently to the door. The hair on his back bristled as he let out a soft growl. I walked over quietly in my bare feet. Muffled knocking like a gloved fist broke the spell.

The fisheye lens of my peephole fanned out a distorted image of two figures, a tall one in a black baseball cap and a shorter one in a hood. They were both wearing skull half-face ski masks. I muffled my own scream. Max started barking and growling. The men disappeared.

Pushing the door open, I stepped squarely on a folded envelope. I carried it inside, opened it, and froze.

I dropped the note to the floor and leaned against the door frame in a cold sweat. *Deep breath. You got this, Sophie. You must be on to something.* I started to reach down again for it but remembered the whole thing about fingerprints.

I called Jeb and then Byron. They arrived with the police in minutes followed by Dot and her team. They lifted fingerprints from the door. None of them were useful. I told them I thought the men wore gloves. My descriptions weren't groundbreaking either, but were consistent with the other sighting of the fleeing arson suspects. One of the neighbors said they saw a black car speeding from our building, one of a million.

Argh. Dot arranged for me to receive protection from the police. The arsonists apparently did not like a journalist looking into the fires. Byron stayed. In the morning I realized he had stayed there on my hard kitchen floor all night.

WE'RE ALL CAREGIVERS

cooked eggs for Byron and then convinced him to go home. I holed up with Max in the apartment. I locked my bedroom door. I tried to work on some other stories. Byron called mid-morning to check in. He then came over and installed some sort of small cameras outside my apartment; he knew what he was doing.

"Let's get you out of here," he said.

We went for lunch and just hung out. Byron invited me to meet up with him at Julie's hospital the next day. There, Julie would help me learn more about Serving Differently at the hospital.

"I'll be there too," Byron said.

I got to the hospital an hour early. When I asked for Julie and Byron, I was escorted by one of Julie's puzzled colleagues to a small procedure room. I knocked and looked in the quasi-operating room to see Byron waving me in with his usual smile. Most of Byron's lower body was covered with a green drape. Julie had on a surgical mask and was wielding a scalpel and something that looked like tweezers while her assistant held a small ultrasound machine. I only know that because I used my super reporter skills and read the label on the machine. Julie was concentrating and did not look up.

Byron insisted, "It's okay, come on in."

I was pretty sure it wasn't okay, but I went inside. Byron had a small stainless steel bowl. Once he saw I was not going to faint, he held the bowl out for me to look. In the bottom were what I could only describe as misshapen BB pellets, tiny bits of wire, and other metal objects. There was blood.

Byron swirled the bowl around, and it made metal-on-metal scraping noises.

"I give up. What are those?"

"Souvenirs, you might say. It's the small scraps of metal that were blown into me. When pieces work their way out and become a nuisance, I head over to Julie. She needs the practice." Julie's eyes furrowed above the mask. "She numbs me up and takes the pieces out. That's my collection so far. I keep it in case I set some sort of record."

The look on my face told him he'd gotten the reaction he was looking for. He smiled, "I still don't know what I'm going to do with them all, they're too small for jewelry." He handed me the silver bowl. I held it, imagining the forces it took to drive these deep into my friend.

Ever the teacher, Byron said, "You know, Sophie, the word 'blood' is part of our word for blessings. Sometimes good can come with blood. Take my man Jesus. He bled out for us. I know what that looks like."

He never stops.

Julie looked up. "We're all done here. I'm sorry, Sophie. I thought we'd be finished by the time you got here. Let's go outside so Byron can get dressed." She stripped off her green surgical gown and washed up. Once she was clean, she hugged me and guided me into a busy hospital hallway.

A few minutes later, Byron came out like this was an everyday occurrence. "I'm going to get back to The House.

Sophie, have a good time with Julie." He set off without a trace of a limp, maybe because we were watching.

"Tough guy," I said to Julie.

"Yes and no. Byron has a soft heart. I really love him." I wondered how she meant it.

We found our way into a conference room beside a busy nurse's station in the Surgical Intensive Care Unit Suite. Julie explained that this was a series of interlocking ICUs. The Pediatric ICU was downstairs. Once seated at the conference table, Julie switched into briefing mode.

"There are a good number of House alumni who work here. The House leaders thought this would be a good place to learn more about Serving Differently.

"My surgical fellowship mentor here, Dr. Parker, believes in helping us set high shared goals, then making a way for us to do better for our patients. We call it goal setting and goal getting."

"How do goal setting and goal getting work at The House?"

She laughed. "At The House, we start every year by setting challenging ministry goals for all of us as leaders, even those of us who are part time. We set goals together and commit to helping each other achieve them. Then we set goals for our student and community work. Our goals are 'hard, specific, clear, and high purpose.' That's part of Why-Power. We then develop people by putting them in situations that allow them to act as a team to achieve stretch goals. We set to work to help them achieve those goals. That's Way-Power."

"That sounds business-like for a ministry," I observed.

"It's a process that works well in businesses, faith-based organizations like The House, or even hospitals." Julie stood up and wrote "Why-Power" on a well-used whiteboard. She avoided erasing some long chemical symbols and equations.

"We have a few Serving Leader exercises we use to set our high purpose goals. One exercise is naming what matters most every step of our work together. We identify personal and group goals. All of this is guided by our values. Jesus said, 'Where your treasure is, there will your heart be also,' meaning what we value can guide our lives. Why-Power is activated when a servant leader works to connect every person on the team to the heart-centric reasons why their work counts. Connect means providing rich, near real-time feedback on the effect of a person's work on teammates and those they serve. It means providing the significance of a teammate's work, showing cause and effect lines of impact. In some jobs, this is not easy. Around here we say: 'We're all caregivers, all of us.' That connects us all to 'Way.'"

Next, she wrote the word 'Way-Power' on the board. "Language is a very specific way we help our teammates. We do exercises to help us consciously salt our conversations with positive, encouraging language. Phrases like 'you've done this before,' 'let's explore that,' and 'I'll help' remind others that they can achieve. We practice, practice, practice the words we choose to use because words matter. Evidence-based research on the brain says when we focus on problems we react with fight, flight, or freeze. To counter that, we pause and talk about 'what we really want' and the 'choices we can make to get there.'"

Evidence-based research on the brain says when we focus on problems we react with fight, flight, or freeze. To counter that, we pause and talk about 'what we really want' and the 'choices we can make to get there.'

As we were speaking a few doctors and other medical professionals walked in. They sat, sipping coffee and nodding along to what Julie was saying. After we finished our discussion, Julie introduced us. One of the nurses, Mary Newman, asked me, "How can we help you, Sophie?"

"I'm in learning mode. Could one of you give a specific example of 'Serving Differently' from your work?"

Doctor Joel Crawford, head of the Pediatric Intensive Care Unit, spoke up with a grin. "We serve each other on the team in order to better serve our patients. When we work together, we can achieve so much more."

"OK," I said, motioning for him to go on. He didn't need the encouragement.

"We had a young girl here last year in the Pediatric Intensive Care Unit who was hurt in a house fire on her family's farm north of Pittsburgh. She was burned on over seventy percent of her body, had serious lung damage, and a damaged heart. We were all determined to save her." The clinicians sat up straighter, engaged. They could not have known how challenging this would be for me. Julie knew and squeezed my hand.

Mary Newman, the critical care nurse added, "Saving her turned out to be hard."

Joel continued, "This badly burned little girl presented a whole host of problems, and we went to work addressing all of them. We designed new technology, modified heart pumps, used new skin regenerative techniques, and applied a lot of love and care."

Mary smiled, "Our girl called herself a 'cowgirl.' Every day that she was alert, she talked about the calf she was raising. She loved that calf. It was becoming a cow without her. We tried video, but she wanted to see that cow in person, so to speak. So we plotted and scoped out a courtyard adjacent to the PICU. It was perfect."

I couldn't imagine where this was going.

"We didn't exactly get permission, so you can't write about this. We wired the courtyard at night with electricity, added life support technology, and created a temporary Peds ICU."

"Outside?"

"You bet! Where there's a will ... well, you know. Then we got the cow there. Cows are big. We snuck Cowgirl down for a no-moon evening visit. Our cowgirl got to be with her cow and the family. That was medicine for her and us. None of us learned this in school."

"For real?"

"Want to see the cow?" Mary pulled out her phone. Yep, there was a cow outside in a makeshift ICU.

I found out Cowgirl was home now and doing okay. The fire did not win. The team and the Cowgirl won. When it was just me and Julie, she checked in.

"How are you doing?"

"That was tough."

"I guessed it would be." She put both arms around me and hugged me tight.

"Thank you, Julie. Is there more?"

"One of the ways a servant leader exercises what we call Way-Power is coaching. When you become a partner-coach with a colleague, you stop telling people what to do. That puts all the pressure on you to come up with all the answers. A servant leader as a coach helps others to think for themselves. With a respectful coaching process, a Serving Leader thinks collaboratively with a teammate."

I nodded and Julie continued, "Our head of nursing on the Pediatric Intensive Care Unit is a colleague. We were going to do a servant leader coaching session. We both would be delighted for you to sit in."

As if on cue, Julie's colleague, Maria Martin, walked in. She looked so young. How could she be the head of nursing for the PICU?

"So Maria: last time we met, we agreed that both of us were going to think about the challenges we're having with clinical rounding at the PICU. What have you got?"

"I've got some ideas."

"Okay, let's start with outcomes. What matters most here?"

"We can do more with rounding. It's clear that the best care comes from multiple disciplines working as a team. We're not there, starting with our rounding process."

"OK, let me just make sure I'm hearing you correctly. The goal is better integrated rounding?"

"Yes." Maria got up and put an outcome statement on the whiteboard.

Our goal is to provide great care for kids starting with better integrated rounding. She added Synergy and Teamwork.

"So, what have you tried?"

"Well, I've tried a few things."

"You can build on small successes. Tell me more."

"Well, we started rounding more with one of our clinical pharmacologists. Our clinical pharmacologists really know the drugs. They think with us, change meds on the spot, try new stuff, and make small adjustments. We make better decisions on the spot. I can keep a clinical pharmacologist busy all the time."

"Great. So let's build on that. What other specialists do you wish you had around?"

"We can always use more real-time input from pulmonology. The kids often have serious lung issues. I thought about maybe bringing them in electronically through an iPad, but I can't seem to get it approved."

"Okay, that's a good idea and also a barrier. Let's talk about that barrier later." Julie wrote down the words

barrier and *electronic availability* on the whiteboard.

"Since you mentioned barriers, is it okay if I bring up another barrier?" Maria asked. "It's a little sensitive."

"Sensitive is okay. And of course you know that this conversation stays in this room, so you don't have to worry about this getting out." They looked at me.

"Yeah, I promise."

Maria said, "It's just that some of the younger docs rotating in and helping lead rounds are in a bit of a hurry. I don't know that they really listen so well to the nurses, the families or patients. We get the sense that they don't really want to partner with us."

"Well that's a barrier for sure," Julie agreed. They put up on the whiteboard

Opportunity — how could rounding work better?

Julie then asked, "Any more successes, Maria?"

"I've been teaching our nurses how to have better deliberations and discussions with all clinical professionals. Nurses sometimes just wait for someone to tell them what to do. I'm encouraging them to be confident clinical professionals and engage in deliberation with their colleagues."

Julie looked thoughtful, then said, "This is jumping ahead to 'ideas and commitments,' but what would be wrong with asking some of your nurses to lead the rounding?"

"Well, that's not how we do things here."

"I know, but *I'm just exploring.*"

I listened to their discussion for another half hour or so.

They agreed to pilot nurse-led rounding. On the issue of virtually bringing in additional clinical expertise during rounding, they decided to approach IT and ask them if it would be possible to electronically bring in consultations from low availability areas. They were going to approach IT together to back each other up and present a united front. At the end, the women prayed for each other, the kids on the unit, and the team.

"Sophie, keep this," Julie said, handing me an outline of their serving leader coaching.

Serving Leader Coaching Basics

Clarify Outcomes:	What is the greater goal you would like to accomplish?	
Reflection & Idea Generation:	Leveraging Existing Success:	Breaking Through Barriers & Building Bridges:
	What have you tried so far? What is working?	What barriers stand in your way? What ideas do you have that would lead to breakthroughs?
Commitment Setting:	What first actions will you take? When?	
Celebration & Acceleration:	Where can we apply the insights from our conversation elsewhere to teach others?	

Julie explained, "The goal is to be a thinking partner — someone who helps the other person develop the solutions and innovations themselves — rather than being an answer dispenser. We have an expanded version, but this was all I could fit on the card.

"Will you come to The House tomorrow? I'm starting some vacation time, but I'm using it at The House."

TWO MINUTE DRILL

got a good night's sleep. I was even up before Darcy, the early riser. I moved through my morning rituals; blueberry shake, exercise, play with Max, and check the to-do list. "Today I'm going to be super-reporter," I told Max. He still had no comment.

I pulled on a pair of jeans and told Max, "*Hasta la vista, baby.*"

Downstairs, I noticed the police car across the street. My hands shook as I texted a 'thank you' to Dot. I punched Sam into the street. Something was different about the ambient light as I drove to The House.

Steel mills are long gone from Pittsburgh. In some atmospheric science kind of way, that has ushered more daylight into the 'Burgh. A scripture came effortlessly into my brain: 'The light shines in the darkness, and the darkness has not overcome it. *La luz resplandece en las tinieblas, y las tinieblas no prevalecieron contra ella.*'

Julie was on the wide front porch watching for me. I got a hug. She took me to where Luke, Byron, and Jeb were in the kitchen, eating leftover pizza from the firehouse for breakfast. Ugh, cold pizza for breakfast. *¡Qué asco!* Luke steered all of us to The Table, which had been mostly decluttered and recently polished. Even the smell was good.

"Sophie, we heard you had an interesting visit to the hospital," Luke said.

Byron laughed, "I got to show Sophie my heavy metal collection. She didn't pass out."

"Let's get started." Luke looked around and asked, "Who wants to pray to start us?" Then, thinking more on the subject, he said, "You know what? I'll start us off."

Luke prayed for "wisdom, protection from evil and distractions, and that God would enjoy our meeting." I wondered if God enjoyed the meetings in which I didn't give Him a thought.

"Sophie, this is the nuts and bolts of disciple-making." He flipped open a well-worn brown Bible. "As Jesus was leaving the Earth, he charged his friends with the 'big mission.' It was to go and make disciples everywhere and teach them."

Julie said with a smile, "Or '*as you go*' in the Greek, right?"

Luke nodded, "Yep."

Byron turned to me, "Knows Greek, but I'm still helping her with Pittsburghese."

Luke continued, "As we go on campus and in the community, we remember that Jesus poured himself into his followers, who weren't much different from us."

"Scary," Byron said, "it's up to us ruffians."

Luke pressed on. "So what was He doing? He was loving them and helping them to practice all that he said and did himself. He saw them as capable, then served them by equipping them. Then he gave them his mission to replicate the same discipleship. That mechanism, disciples forming more disciples, is God's way to grow His church. It's up to us now."

I watched as each member of the leadership team seemed to newly consider this. One at a time, they nodded in agreement with Luke. It was solemn even with cold pizza crusts in hand.

I turned to Byron and asked, "What does this look like for you day-to-day?"

"As-you-go disciple formation for us in part means doing projects on campus and in the community with our students while we sharpen each other. We call these 'Kingdom Ventures.' We try to do some good for others and *work with each other* to grow as disciples. The firehouse does the same thing."

"Only we get to drive fast with the siren and lights on," Jeb said.

"Julie," Luke prompted, "can you speak to this for Sophie?"

Julie thought for a second. "I'm discipling a group of students, most of whom are headed on to medicine or other health professions. We follow the same servant leadership and disciple formation process. The theme of our Kingdom Venture work is the 'healing ministry of Jesus.' We volunteer to help the frail, elderly, and the vulnerable in the community. We check on them, pray with them, and deliver simple care. We practice the concepts of 'See and Serve Differently' in very practical ways. It's my favorite thing in life, and I hope to continue this back in China. Byron is going to come and help."

Byron nodded a slight yes and picked up, "'And there's more,' as they say on late-night TV. We do a ton of outreach with international students. We use the same discipleship and leadership process. I plan to go overseas next year to encourage some of my students."

Luke announced, "Okay, caffeine time. Sophie, you first. I need another minute with the team. Byron says you have a refined coffee palate. We managed to get some coffee that we hope you will like." Luke smiled broadly.

I walked to the kitchen. I wasn't alone. There were two massive students in torn jeans and Pitt t-shirts crammed into the small kitchen. They were the twins from the teaching event and the women's shelter presentation. They effectively blocked my path to the coffee. I waited for them to finish and the two began to wander away, coffee and books in hand.

"I'm Sophie Alsas," sticking out my hand. "I'm doing a story on The House. May I ask you a couple of questions?"

"Of course," the two replied perfectly in sync. They sat at the kitchen table, causing their chairs to creak in protest.

"So who are you again?"

"I'm Jaden. I saw you at the mayor's office."

"And I'm Cam. I'm younger by five minutes. Better looking, though. We were recruited here for football. We could've gone a lot of places, but Jaden knew a girl here."

"Anyway, we're linebackers." Jaden moved the conversation on, frowning at Cam.

"I assume you are part of The House programs?"

"You bet," both said again in perfect unison.

I made a note mostly to emphasize that they were on the record.

"How has The House has affected you?"

Cam said, "It's changed our lives. Neither of us were what you'd call strong Christians. We mostly lived for football."

Jaden added, "When Coach heard we were coming to The House, he encouraged us. Coach speaks pretty openly about character and about Christ. You'll probably see him around. We get a lot of encouragement from him and some of our teammates. We're athletes," Jaden continued, "If we don't work out on our own in the offseason, running and hitting the weights, then we won't perform at top level."

Cam completed the thought: "It's the same for us spiritually. If we don't put in the work to memorize scripture, pray, and stay in community with other Christians, we won't be ready. We don't want to lose."

He frowned, looking at my notebook: "You haven't written much down."

"I'm absorbing, that's all. It's good stuff, guys. What do you want me to write down? I've got two minutes."

They exchanged non-verbal twin signals. Cam said, "Great! A two-minute drill run by the defense!" With that, the twins went into hurry-up mode. I kept up somehow but couldn't get who said what. They just volleyed remarks back and forth. The House leadership team filtered in quietly to get their coffee, letting the twins keep the center stage. Here's what I got down:

> *"The scriptures we memorize come to help us when we most need them. In the weight room, in games, we're not alone. Christ is with us. Win or lose, even when we personally screw up, we know we're totally loved. Prayer keeps us centered."*

Then they sped up even more and started quoting scripture back and forth. It seemed like there was some competition between them.

"I can do all things through Him who strengthens me."
"PHILIPPIANS 4:13."

"Do not fear, for I am with you. Do not be dismayed, for I am your God."
"ISAIAH 41:10."

If one said the verse, the other gave the reference.

*"Therefore there is now no condemnation for those who
are in Christ Jesus."*
"ROMANS 8:1."

*"Therefore, if anyone is in Christ, the new creation has come:
The old has gone, the new is here!"*
"2 CORINTHIANS 5:17."

*"And let us run with perseverance the race marked out for us,
fixing our eyes on Jesus, the pioneer and perfecter of faith."*
"HEBREWS 12:1-2."

*"Come, follow me," Jesus said, "and I will send you out
to fish for people."*
"MATTHEW 4:19."

They knew their scripture.

Luke finally interrupted them. "Okay yinz guys, let Sophie go. We need her back." As I started to go, Cam stopped me and put a big paw on my shoulder. "Next time we see you, we want to hear your verse of the week." I now knew that the 'verse of the week' was a thing.

"Okay," I stammered, afraid of letting these giants down. I'd better get a verse. I said goodbye and squeezed around them.

Back in the other room, Luke had a book out on The Table to show me. "This is Dallas Willard's *Divine Conspiracy.* 'His plan is for us to develop, as apprentices to Jesus, to the point where we can take our place in the ongoing creativity of the universe.'[7]... 'The intention of God is that we should

---

7   Willard. *The Divine Conspiracy,* 378

each become the kind of person whom he can set free in the universe.'[8] He sees us as we are and how we will be. He aims to set us free with power and earned responsibility."[9]

Byron took over. "He wants us to be *free* and *prepared*. He's got work for us to do here, and I expect a lot more to come. We'll join Him in the ongoing, team-oriented, delightful, creative work of managing His great kingdom forever." Then he said, like it just occurred to him, "Hey, want to come to breakfast at Ritter's with me and Jeb? Say 0700? We need somebody to pay."

---

8   Ibid, 279.
9   Ibid, 39.

DANGER CLOSE

got to breakfast at Ritter's on Baum at 7:15, almost on time, but my hair was super messy and my Steelers t-shirt was the one I slept in. Byron seemed determined to make a morning person out of me.

Nope.

Pittsburgh's go-to classic diner was filled with Shadyside Hospital nurses coming off the night shift. I quickly spotted the guys, already seated with their elbows on the table and mugs of coffee in hand, leaning in towards one another across the table. I got my own mug of diner coffee. My need for caffeine outweighed my taste preferences this morning. As I slid in with my own mug, Jeb stood, the West Virginia gentleman. Byron looked up at Jeb, a little bemused.

"Sorry," Byron said, "I'm untrained."

To make up for it, he gave me a big Byron hug.

After sitting down, I decided to bring up something that had been bothering me for a while. "Guys, can I just say I think you two are still just a little bit too perfect for my story. You each told me stuff off the record. What about something I could print?"

They looked at each other and nodded at some secret agreement. Jeb spoke, "Byron and I aren't just buddies, we're accountability partners. You can print that."

"What does that mean?"

"Well, you know I dropped out of college in large part because of my drinking. Truth be told, I had a real problem. I needed help."

Byron put his hand on Jeb's forearm and continued the confession. "I'm one of Jeb's accountability partners. I help him stay sober."

"I also have an AA sponsor, but Byron and I focus on the spiritual side of why I'm drawn to alcohol."

Byron nodded. "The accountability isn't one-sided. Jeb helps me. After my injuries, I became dependent on painkillers. The drugs kept the pain but not the PTSD at bay. Luke helped me realize that the drugs were taking control. I'm seeing a counselor. Julie's helping me dial back on my meds. Jeb's my accountability partner. Write about this if you want."

"I will work it in. What are you guys up to this morning?"

Byron slid a piece of paper toward me and inverted it so I could read. I saw a well-used version of The House community discipleship practices.

Community Practices:

We seek to live in the way of Jesus by practicing simple weekly rhythms — to regularly...

Listen **God**
We seek to practice listening by setting aside focused time devoted to list to God's "still, small voice." *Romans 10:17*

Learn from God
We seek to practice learning by devoting at least 1 focused time of learning, from Christ, through scripture each week.
Proverbs 6:21

Eat with others
We strive to eat with at least 2 people we don't live with (1 from the The House and 1 not) each week.

Encourage others
We seek to practice encouragement by intentionally encouraging 2 people (1 from the The House and 1 not) through words, gifts or actions each week.
Yes!

Give ourselves away to the world
We look for regular ways to give away our time, money, skills and/or passions to others and the world.

Jeb explained, "We do these iron sharpening iron breakfasts all the time. We already checked in on the sobriety front."

Byron added, "It's not what we do or who we are at the moment alone that counts. It's what we will become that also lasts forever."

For the next hour, it was a buddy movie. The guys helped each other figure out how to better implement each practice. They laughed and drank about a gallon of coffee, somehow managing to get two of the waitresses to pay them a lot of attention.

Finally, Jeb turned to me. "Luke asked me to set up a time for you to learn from our friends Matt and Elizabeth Richard. They are great, real pros at Why-Power. They help students know God and challenge them to answer some of the big questions concerning why they should serve."

I took a quick break, not wanting to miss too much. I visited the restroom and splashed my face with cold water, still trying to wake up. By the time I got back, they were talking about 'listening to God.' This is a real subject?

Byron said to Jeb, "God communicates regularly with those living and working with Him, just as we regularly communicate with the people we live and work with. How do you hear God, Jeb?"

Jeb answered in his typical matter-of-fact manner. "I hear God in the scriptures I'm reading and memorizing. I also hear Him in my own thoughts." Jeb turned to me to explain. "I've learned to recognize God's unique voice in my thoughts, usually in things that I wouldn't think of myself. Sometimes I hear Him in the voices of my friends — once in a while from you, Byron. I even hear Him speaking in some of the things I say to other people. It still surprises me."

As a kid, I really believed that God could "speak" to people like this. Now I'm hearing it all again.

"Why do you want to hear from God?" Byron asked, steering Jeb's attention.

"He's my friend and my Lord. We're working together, and like you said, why wouldn't He helpfully communicate with me on what we are doing together? I want that."

"What's your favorite thing to hear from God?"

"Well, it's all good, but I like that He tells me how much I'm loved just the way I am. Sometimes we're just quiet with each other."

I had never heard this kind of talk from people my age. If this was Christianity, it was more radical than I expected. That actually drew me in.

"But the quiet times are most rare these days with all the fires."

"Yeah, that's hard, man. I know what that's like. But God's still with you even when you don't get those quiet moments together."

"Wait," I interrupted, "are there any new developments with the arsons I should know about?" I had to know if there was any new information.

"Not really. We're still getting suspicious fires. It's wearing on me and the team." As he spoke, Jeb's demeanor changed, his face toughening. Jeb glanced at me and then addressed his friend. "Byron, the fires are deliberate and targeted. Someone is still trying to hurt us." Jeb turned to face me. "They are getting more clever, Sophie. Do you want us to talk about something else?"

I shook my head for them to go on, but I was sick with anxiety. I cared. Not for a long time, but again I cared.

"Byron, we're being hunted," Jeb said.

Byron reached across the table and gripped both of Jeb's forearms, hard. "Been there, man. You've got to stay focused. If something seems off, it is. Get out! You did it last time. I know this feels like a physical fight. But this is also a spiritual fight. 'Take up the whole armor of God. Stand your ground. Do not yield an inch.'"

I was done. I went home and worked on other stories for the paper.

Fear chewed on me.

JOURNEYS

wasn't ready to work, but it was time to meet some friends of The House, the Richards. Luke wasn't able to come, but Matt and Elizabeth Richard and Jeb were all coming to my place. Max stayed close to me as I buzzed around my apartment.

Jeb got to my place first.

"Thanks for coming, Jeb. How are you doing?"

"Pretty good, I guess," he replied with a tired smile.

"You guess?"

"It takes a lot to be ready for a trap on any run. I'm doing pretty good though."

Max let me know that my other guests were at the door with a happy bark. How do dogs know the difference between the good guys and the bad guys?

Matt and Elizabeth Richard came right in and made themselves at home. Actually, they made me at home in my own home. They brought coffee, healthy snacks, and energy. Hospitality was apparently typical of the Richards. Matt offered me French press coffee to drink and suggested dried African dates to go along with it. Darcy, who was home for the morning, took it all in and decided on the spot to sit in on the interview. I would never have predicted that.

I got right to it.

"Matt and Elizabeth: why are you here?" Darcy laughed at my directness.

"Well," Matt replied, munching on a date, "we're here to talk to you about Why-Power Journeys."

"Okay. What's a Journey in this context?" I asked.

Matt stood like he was on stage. He apparently had to move to communicate. "We take students to live in marginalized communities in global megacities all over the world. Students and staff live together and intentionally explore what serving looks like outside the U.S. We talk to leaders from all walks of life in these megacities. We learn practices of serving from these leaders around the world. One intent is for students to learn from people who are different from them. The big intent is for them to answer the big whys for their own lives. Our role is to facilitate the experience and let God do His thing, to connect them to Him."

"Right," Elizabeth chimed in, smiling at her animated husband. "A lot of students come to us trained to think of this as a missions program where they're going to be the experts telling the locals what to do. They believe they're going to rescue people in bad circumstances. We think the Journey is about seeing and serving differently."

"Really?" Darcy inquired.

"Yes," Elizabeth replied. "Being a disciple involves seeing the poor differently. We think you can develop an enduring connection to God's purposes if you are willing to listen to and learn from those you want to help. Much of the time when we see a poor community, we wrongly think that they don't have or know much. So students think their time with us will involve telling people what to do and giving them stuff."

Matt added, "Journey students come see people in poor places as smart, hard-working, and creative. The students learn from the locals how they work creatively with the assets they already have. We call it 'Building on Assets!'"

Elizabeth continued, "This really challenges our students because most of them come from relatively wealthy cultures that believe poor people are somehow deficient. The reality is people in these global communities can solve many of their problems on their own. If we see this reality over there, our students can continue to see differently back here. That's the hope."

"I think I get it," I said.

Matt continued, "So the in-country service opportunities for students come up after they've actually listened to the community. Students learn to take their cues from the local leaders."

"Do you have an example?" Darcy asked, joining me as an interviewer. *Nice!*

"Sure," Matt answered. "One time, after weeks with students on site, the community asked us, 'Can you tear down that building the other missionaries built? It's ugly and we don't know why it's there.' The group before us missed the mark. Listening to the community, we learned what they really wanted our help with. Once we had the direction from the community on what to do, students took charge of the tear-down process. They also talked to the community leaders to learn what the community really wanted in place of the building. Listening to the community was key. We didn't want to put something in place of that building only for the community to ask the next group to tear it down as well. We became relevant by listening."

Darcy was engaged. "What does this look like for the students? How can students listen if they don't speak the language?"

"Sometimes there is a language barrier," Elizabeth acknowledged. "In other places, students speak the language. Everywhere we go, there's at least one person in the community who speaks English. But students benefit by learning to connect with others without using words. You know, God doesn't just use words to communicate with us."

I followed up: "Discipleship is the big 'why' at The House. How does the Journey help?"

Matt responded, "Most students go on a Journey to grow in their relationship with Jesus in difficult circumstances. The average college student doesn't get this chance."

Elizabeth nodded, "In terms of discipleship, maybe as an example, I can share a little bit about how my Journey influenced me. For me, both as a student and now a faculty member, Journeys have made me a better Serving Leader — I use the term serving on purpose — and a more intentional disciple-maker. When I first did a Journey as a student, a big question on my own mind was about the character of God. Does God know about what's wrong with the world? There are hard things going on all around. Does God care?"

"I've had that question since my dad died," I admitted.

Elizabeth's face softened. "I got some of this answered for me on my Journey. Leaders and locals helped me see that God is indeed there and that He cares. I saw hard things worked out for good even in my own life."

"Like what?" I asked, curious about where she saw God in all the brokenness.

"So, one way I saw God working on my Journey was when I broke my leg while hiking. We were climbing through a ravine in Wadi Rum, and I slipped and fell, breaking both my tibia and fibula. With my leg in a cast, I was limited to crutches and was unable to go on the next trip the group had to a city in the north where we would need to do a lot of walking. Instead, I had to stay in Ramala by myself. I was so disappointed that was I going to miss some of the homestays, learning, and adventures my group was going to have without me. I was mad at God for letting me get hurt and ruining my experience. What happened instead was that I got to stay with a local woman, Noor, who took me to her church and her work. I learned so much from Noor and really got to see what leadership as a woman in an Islamic country was like. I also got to spend extra time with the intern, Sari, who was asked to stay back with me. My time with Sari was transformational as well. Sari let me participate and learn about what it meant to be an intern and work on a Journey. My time with Sari led me to apply for a job with Journey, and here I am. The broken leg that I thought was keeping me back from my adventures actually led me to my current adventure. God used my literal brokenness to help me find meaning — and eventually, my husband."

She smiled at Matt, who added, "Yeah. we met just two years later in Cairo."

"So I got to see God take a bad situation and turn it into something beautiful. I wouldn't say that the broken leg or being left behind wasn't extremely difficult. It was tough, and God brought me to Matt and to my calling because of my fall. And my experience of being mentored by Sari along with the Journey fostered in me a deep desire to help students experience God and His care. Students get to see God at work in every kind of neighborhood and join Him. As a result, many students choose to join God in His purpose for the world. Because of the Journeys I'm more determined to continue to grow and join Jesus in His work today. I have my 'why' do this work. Why Power."

"What are ways students see this played out in local communities?" I asked.

Elizabeth stood and moved over to the refrigerator.

"I've got a story," she said.

We watched her pour clear water into her glass. She was on stage now.

"One of our partners in Mexico City is in a poor neighborhood. They didn't have clean running water." She held the clear glass up to the light. "While we were there, the government made the neighborhood an offer. If the community bought land for a water tower, the government would build it. We were thinking, 'These poor people will never be able to buy this land. This is a trick.'

"But that became their 'why work together,' and the community totally organized to find a way. They prayed together and approached everyone who would benefit. They asked even the poorest people for donations. We prayed and worked with them. In just three months, this very poor community had all the funds they needed. They all went together to the city hall and bought the land. What a day that was." Elizabeth took a drink of water.

Matt smiled and added, "The government built the tower. The community now has running water and a monument to a shared greater goal. Our students got to see something extraordinary, a community rallying behind a shared goal."

Elizabeth put her arm around her husband. "Matt thought it would at least take a year."

The couple shared a smile and a hug. Clearly, these two loved each other. Elizabeth continued, "There were two gifts that came from this experience. One was the water tower, and the other was the community's realization that, yes, we can do this. We have Why-Power and Way-Power if we work together on greater goals. This realization has spurred even more community work. They've installed public art throughout the neighborhood. Crime has dropped, drugs have disappeared, and the churches that helped with all of this are full again."

My stomach growled, prompting a smile from Darcy. "Sounds like Sophie's hungry."

Matt glanced at his phone. "No wonder, it's already one o'clock. Let us take you to lunch. We can go to Noodlehead and keep talking."

"How about I meet you there," I suggested. "I need to talk to Max." Puzzled looks ensued. "I mean, I need to walk my dog."

"I'd love to come to lunch too if that's ok, I just need to grab my climbing stuff so I can head to the gym after," Darcy announced.

"Great!" Matt and Elizabeth replied in unison. My skeptical roommate was in.

"Hey Sophie, mind if I come 'talk to Max' too?" Jeb said with a smile.

"I think that'd be ok," I replied. "Right, Max?" Max barked in agreement.

Leash in hand, Jeb and I walked Max down to the sidewalk.

"Tell me about Max," Jeb asked as we paused for him to sniff a few bushes.

"I got Max when I was in high school, a few months after we moved back from Ecuador. I was having a hard time adjusting to American culture and struggling to make friends. My mom took me to a therapist to help me work through depression and grief. To help with the adjustment, my therapist recommended a dog to help keep me company and provide me something stable to emotionally attach to. A week later, my mom found someone who had golden puppies for adoption. I saw Max and fell in love."

"Wow, like family?"

"Yeah," I nodded. "When I lived in the dorms for my first two years of college, he stayed with Mom, and I'd try to see him as often as possible. He came to live with me once I got my own apartment. What about you, Jeb? Have you had dogs?"

"I love dogs. We had a sheepdog growing up, Trixy. She loved herding us kids around. I've got a memory of her chasing and nipping at me as I was sledding down the hill behind our house. She lived to be fifteen. We also had some outdoor cats that came and went. I remember a Ralph. My sister Lily was as attached to them as I was."

He looked down at Max, who had continued sniffing various things as we walked and now was concentrated on a squirrel at the base of a tree. "One of these days I'd love to get a dog again, but with the station work I'd need to find someone to take care of it while I worked my shifts. You're lucky to have Max."

We finished walking Max and met Darcy on the stairs.

"Do you all want a ride over to Noodlehead?" Jeb asked.

"Thanks, but I need my car to head to the gym after this," Darcy replied.

"I'd love a ride, Jeb," I chimed in. "Let me drop off Max and get my backpack."

"Great, see you all there," Darcy said, swinging her duffle over her shoulder.

A little while later Darcy, Jeb, and I joined the Richards at an industrial style corner table surrounded by exotic plants. We ordered and our Thai food arrived in minutes.

"You know," Jeb spoke up over a steaming bowl of Pad Thai, "Luke from The House did a Journey."

"Really?" I asked.

"Yeah, after his injury he went on a Journey. I believe it helped him find his purpose beyond hockey. He says it deepened his relationship with God and inspired him to work in campus ministry. As you know, Luke wanted to join us, but he's got some seminary stuff today. He wanted me to let you know he's a big fan of Journeys."

"You all are so connected," Darcy observed.

Matt smiled. "It's a God thing. He does that."

I asked, "Matt and Elizabeth, what do you both love about this?"

Matt answered, "We love to see people transform and join God in His kingdom work. Journeys create the space and experiences for transforming and joining. Students and staff can encounter God in very personal and life-changing ways by being in a space where they can grapple with big questions about God and His purpose in the world. They get to experience people who love God, people who tell them they're loved by God, and they actually invite the students to join God in His plans."

Jeb's voice concluded us with a resounding 'Amen!'

"Oh, and Sophie, I almost forgot, but Luke would like me to escort you to a special student commissioning ceremony tomorrow. Can you come? I can drive you," Jeb asked.

"Of course."

To my surprise, Darcy asked, "Can I come too?"

"Of course," Jeb replied in my same tone, making us laugh.

As I was organizing my notes back at home, my phone buzzed with an email from Jeb. I opened it assuming it was an update about the ceremony tomorrow. As I read it, I instantly recognized that Jeb meant this for Byron but instead sent it to me. The mistake was probably because I was the subject.

"Byron, you're right. I'm at that point of no return. I need to admit to Sophie that I'm seriously interested. Advice? See you tonight."

I decided not to respond on the off chance that he wouldn't discover that he sent the email to me and not Byron. I reread it about ten times.

That night in my dreams, someone familiar was holding my hand. He had his sleeves rolled up, and we were walking down one of the Andes foothills in waist-deep maize and flowers. I kept losing my footing, but my companion kept pulling me back up.

COMMISSIONED

The next morning, Jeb picked Darcy and me up in his candy apple Camaro. He made no mention of the email. Embarrassed? Changed his mind? We quickly arrived at The House. Jeb led me to a chapel on the second floor. Stained glass windows on the back of The House and morning sun created a mosaic of colors.

Up front was a rough cross. A cluster of students were writing on small pieces of paper. They nailed them to the cross when they had finished writing.

We slipped in and took seats beside Julie, who whispered, "This is the first part of The Commissioning."

Jeb added, "We do this every year for House students and staff. The first bit is what we call 'The Leave Behind.' We do this throughout the year, but this is the big one. Each person writes down something they want to leave behind as they go out to what's next. That's why we nail it to the cross."

"Like what?" Darcy asked. I couldn't imagine either.

Julie explained, "All sorts of things; sins, idols, emotional baggage. It's whatever slows one down from living the Christian life. People nail to the cross destructive relationships, addictions, habits ... well, you get the idea. Whatever you need to leave behind. Nailing something to the cross means you're giving it to God. I gave Him my sins and my shame."

If only I could do this.

Jeb explained that the next part of the ceremony was for each student to describe why and how they were going to go out into the world.

The students were remarkable. Some were committing to grave risk in living for Christ. These were engineers, computer scientists, nurses, doctors, ROTC students, teachers, artists, missionaries, and writers. There were a good number of international students returning home to serve.

Julie leaned over and whispered, "Alumni of The House are going everywhere. This is what we were working for all this time. They are answering the big questions of why serve and what they will do."

One tiny Sri Lankan girl in particular took my breath away. She was going back to teach in Sri Lanka and would live a hard life. Living as a Christian could get her killed.[10]

"This is what the normal Christian life[11] should look like," Julie responded. "I'm working on my own great purpose talk. I love it here, but I can't wait for what's next." She glanced at Byron.

The last part of the commissioning was encouragement, a charge, and prayer from the staff. Luke encouraged the students to work at their "community practices every day" as they pursue "Christ in the company of friends." Julie charged the students with seeking out "the hurting and the poor to serve them, heal them, and learn from them."

---

10   Zylstra, Sarah Eekhoff, "The Top 50 Countries Where It's Most Dangerous to Follow Jesus." *Christianity Today.* January 10, 2018. http://www.christianitytoday.com/news/2018/january/top-50-christian-persecution-open-doors-world-watch-list.html.

11   Watchman, Nee, *The Normal Christian Life* (Bombay: Gospel Literature), 1957.

Jeb was direct as usual, standing to address the group in his fireman pants and a black t-shirt. "Don't let any habits or dark secrets disqualify you. Confess to your friends and lean on your brothers and sisters. Stay in community with others."

Byron asked the students to take the light of Christ into every dark place in their paths. "Do not be afraid for your needs or your lives. God will provide. He already has a work and home for you." Hand on heart, Byron finished, "If any of you need any of us, we'll be there... anywhere, anytime, for anything. So help me Christ my God."

I stayed in my seat when the commissioning ended. I watched Byron and the other leaders spend time with each student— praying with, hugging, and encouraging them. An hour later, the chapel had emptied out with people headed downstairs to get something to eat at The Table. Darcy followed the crowd in search of food and friends. Byron finished up with the last student and came back to sit next to me.

"What were you saying?"

"Most of it is private, but I did talk about courage. Knowing that God is with you as you go out into the work, gives courage to do what God has called us to do. My verse is Isaiah 41:10, 'So do not fear, for I am with you; do not be dismayed, for I am your God. I will strengthen you and help you; I will uphold you with my righteous right hand.' I learned that verse from one of my Christian brothers in the Helmand Province. He taught me the verse and later showed it in action."

"Action? Is that something you can share?"

"Yeah, sure." He moved me over to the stained glass. "I frankly only remember pieces of it personally, but I got told the whole story by my teammates later. My unit was mixed in with a group of Rangers moving from one part of the city to the other on foot. It was pitch-dark, no moon—our favorite time to move. We rounded a corner, and right in front of us, a hundred meters out, was one of our Humvee vehicles on fire. I thought that some of our guys might be in there, and I guess I took off running for the vehicle. That's really the last thing I actually remember.

"It turned out that it was a captured Humvee that the enemy had set on fire to lure us in. They had rigged IEDs — explosive devices — around the vehicle. I stepped right on one and probably would've bled out right there but my buddy, apparently unafraid that he'd step on another device, ran in to get me. He threw me over his shoulder and ran me back out of the kill zone."

"Oh, wow! Hero!"

"That would embarrass him. Sophie, you've met him."

"I have? When, where?"

"He's a student. He was the guy in the wheelchair that I took coffee to in the quad during our walk. He's my buddy Martinez. Pittsburgh is his hometown. He's the reason I'm here. He got pretty shot up in a firefight a year after my injury. He said that he came home to Pittsburgh so that he could watch out for me."

I was too stunned to speak.

Byron smiled slyly. "Hey, add 'courage' to your story notes, mention Martinez."

That night was a long, dark night of the soul. Mom had let me take the Papa chair to my place, and that's where I sat all night, deciding.

I was charged by Ben with The House story, and it was a good one. I found believers in pursuit of Christ in the company of friends. I discovered a community full of people willing to run toward God when others were running away. Through Jeb and Byron, I learned about courage, serving, and sacrifice. They helped me finally understand my dad. I talked to God about all of this.

And my story?

It's a prodigal daughter deciding whether to stay away or turn back toward home. In the Andes I would often go without shoes. Mostly I wandered. When it was time to come home, I always ran direct and fast.

At first light I left my shoes off. I went down the stairs of my building. I walked the green spaces from my apartment toward The House with the sun creeping up behind me. I knew Byron would be there waiting for me, somehow.

On the way I rehearsed a speech.

In the last mile I really started to run. I was flying. Byron was outside to meet me, a radiant pink and orange sunrise framing The House behind him.

I forgot my rehearsed speech. "Byron, I want to come home."

Byron said, "You're most welcome back, Sophie. You were always God's daughter." As Byron spoke, Luke, Julie, and even Jeb appeared on the porch and quietly joined us. How were they here?

As the morning sun rose higher in the sky Julie, Luke, and Byron peeled off to start their days. Jeb and I sat quietly on the porch sipping the cups of coffee Julie brought out to us on her way to work. There were so many things I wanted to say, but I waited.

HAMMER AND SPIKE

om wanted to celebrate at her place. I had a different idea. Every month at The House, there was a meal followed by a talk and communion in the chapel. I wanted to take communion and celebrate with my friends. Mom agreed to the plan, and I asked Byron to give the talk.

The evening of the dinner, I walked into The House as family. This group of saints and sinners were family.

My childhood Christian community was reforming and coming back for me. This was the feeling of belonging I remembered. In a second I imagined thousands of communities like this all over the world. How could I say this all in my story?

Our meal of lentil soup and rye bread was joyful. I couldn't count the number of hugs, welcomes, and encouragements I got. Jeb and some of his Fire Station 9 teammates were there to hang out until their shift.

After the dinner we shifted to the chapel. Byron spoke from Isaiah 49:16 to the packed room. "I heard Tim Keller in New York speak on a passage from Isaiah. In Isaiah, God's people were feeling alienated from Him. God took the initiative to assure them of his love." Byron seemed to be struggling. He gripped the table edge.

"God said this to His people: 'See, I have engraved you on the palms of my hands.'" Byron rolled up his sleeves and held up his palms. "You might think this is just what God would say. It's a whole lot more. The Hebrew word for 'engrave' here is unique. It indicates the use of a *hammer and chisel* to do the engraving. A hammer and a chisel or a spike.

"Keller said that on rare occasions in ancient times, a servant might mark on his hands the name of his master. But never would a master mark on his hand the names of his subjects. That would indicate a profound commitment of the master to the servant. It just wasn't done. But actually it was done, centuries later. After his resurrection, Jesus appeared to his friend Thomas to show him the deep, painful wounds made in his hands. They were made by Roman spikes and hammer. Jesus did that for us."[12]

Radios among Jeb's team suddenly begin to squawk. Firemen turned the volume down, looking apologetic, but still listening. Looking worried, Byron stopped his talk, apologized, and went over to the firemen's group huddle. I went over too.

Jeb explained, "We have to go, Sophie. Dot's Arson Team has a real time lead and she thinks there might be a major arson about to go down. Sorry, we can't stay."

A visiting pastor from one of our sponsoring churches was hastily engaged to start communion. The firemen took communion first, along with Byron. I noticed Byron took extra. I went next so that my fireman friends could be there with me. But right after I took communion the firemen, along with Byron, disappeared. We were left to pray.

I went home and listened to my scanner. Within an hour I heard the call for Fire Station 9. There was a major fire in a

---

12   Keller, Timothy, "Can a Mother Forget-Tim Keller Sermon Jam". *Youtube video.* Filmed February 2010. Posted September 2014. www.youtube.com/watch?v=or-TWUh72vs&feature=youtu.be.

large paint factory in Larimer Square that lit up the sky. I could see it from my place.

Dear God, please protect Jeb and the team. Help me with my doubts and fears. I called my mom and explained what I had just heard.

"Let me pray, *mi amor.*" My mom prayed with me for Jeb, Byron and the team. As soon as we hung up my phone buzzed. It was Byron. His voice was almost drowned out by the sound of the siren. Bryon knew I would be concerned.

"Sophie, it's a big one. You might want to get over here."

"Byron, I'm terrified."

He said, "Jeb's a smart guy with a great team."

Sam-the-Jeep got me to the warehouse quickly where the fire was already big and dangerous. I spotted some of Jeb's team, put on my press pass, and got as close as I could. I was stopped by Big Mike.

"Sophie, you can't come any closer. Jeb's around back putting water on the warehouse."

"What's in the warehouse?"

Big Mike looked down at his boots, reluctant to answer me. "Tons of paint, chemicals, and other bad stuff. We've got to keep that from going up." He looked up from his boots into my face to see how I was taking it. Not well.

"Why Jeb?"

"He volunteered to go. It's pretty much his tactical job anyway. Look, I gotta go."

This was my worst nightmare. I looked for Byron. I spotted him fifty feet away, ready for action. He saw me staring at him and gave me a thumbs up. Then he was gone. I angled for the on-site commander for more information.

"Is this press business or personal, Sophie?" he asked.

"Personal," I admitted.

"Sophie, this is one tough fire. Jeb's team is working on knocking it down from the north side of the building. If that warehouse goes up we'll have a mess and a real threat to this neighborhood."

I took that in and asked, "I saw Byron head around that way."

"He's the best paramedic we have available. Besides, he wouldn't take no for an answer. So I sent him closer."

"We'll need him," a fireman shouted. "We've got a collapse around back. It's bad."

I dropped to my knees in the mud.

Big Mike pulled me back up. "We've got to work, Sophie. Please move back past the truck."

I retreated back next to another fire command vehicle.

"You! Come here!" One of Jeb's teammates recognized me. He let me listen, but I couldn't understand it all.

I found out later that Jeb and his teammates were pouring water over the top of hundreds of barrels of flammable chemicals. The intense heat melted some metal hooks holding up the roof. The collapse was right on top of where Jeb and several of his teammates were working. I was numb and in shock, but I kept listening.

Radio calls indicated Jeb and the team were still alive but trapped. The fire was gaining momentum with fresh oxygen. The unit needed to pour water in, but with men trapped, there was a real danger of drowning the team.

A rescue was organized quickly. Power equipment was used to lift steel and blocks from on top of the men. The first few were rescued quickly, but one remained trapped under a cross-shaped steel support structure.

It was Jeb.

Jeb's teammates wrapped me in a blanket because I was shivering and could not stop. Then I heard Byron's calm voice over the radio: "He's wedged in there. We can't get the hydraulic jack in."

There was muffled talk I could not make out and another voice took over.

"Byron's got a plan. He's going to squeeze through and help Jeb. He's insisting."

The site commander grabbed the mic. "Put him on."

"Are you sure, Byron?" he asked.

I heard Byron's voice respond: "I can get him out."

"We're going to get you a little further back," Big Mike told me. I knew he just didn't want me to hear any more. They were walking me back when we heard the incredible explosion. I don't recall passing out, but I did. I woke up in an emergency vehicle with Jeb's teammates at Julie's hospital. They helped me to a waiting area outside of Critical Care. It was there that Jeb's teammates told me the rest of the story.

Jeb had been trapped, but Byron somehow got to Jeb and freed him. Once freed, Byron pushed Jeb out to the rescue team.

There was a mighty explosion, and the entire remainder of the wall fell in.

Jeb survived. Byron did not.

HOUSE ON FIRE

B yron's death brought shock and community-wide grief. The story of his final minutes was told over and over. No one could explain how Byron was able to lift the huge beam to rescue Jeb.

For the second time in my life, I was dealing with loss. I was also dealing with the guilt I felt for being glad that Jeb was spared. Mom and I talked, walked, cried, and prayed until three in the morning. I wasn't angry with God. I knew where Byron was, but I missed my friend just like I missed my dad.

Julie was grief stricken. The two of them were indeed exploring a relationship. We helped each other.

The next day was filled with preparations for Byron's memorial and funeral. Spec Ops teammates from all over the military poured in. One unit drove up from Fort Bragg, North Carolina. They were different. The firefighter and paramedic communities came together to honor one of their own. Pitt and Carnegie Mellon students held their own immediate prayer vigil in The House chapel. The Table downstairs was covered with a hundred photos of Byron, illustrating a story of a life well lived.

On the third night Byron's body was laid in one of Pittsburgh's historic stone churches for a closed-casket memorial service. I met Byron's parents at the church standing next to their fallen son. His mom, who was in military uniform, and his dad, a retired pastor, were keeping up a brave front. They were at the center of hundreds of grieving students, combat veterans, firemen, and paramedics. His combat veteran teammates described the many times Byron had rushed into the danger zone to rescue others, even some of them. Jeb was a silent presence at these conversations. I could not draw him out. No one could imagine life without Byron.

That night after the service, the Fort Bragg unit stayed all night as an honor guard. I stayed too. One member of the team, "Dog," who apparently knew Byron well, said to me, "He was always there for us. We wanted to be here for his family."

His fire department and military friends decided on a plan to carry Byron all the way to the cemetery the final morning. The mayor and others helped make this possible. The church was miles away from the cemetery. New bearers took over every block. At intersections fire trucks with crossed ladders arched above the marchers. No one in Pittsburgh complained about the road closures. For the last few blocks, Byron's closest friends carried the casket. I walked with Jeb.

The service was outdoors in the Homewood cemetery. There was a crowd. The American flag over his coffin was a special flag that his unit had flown in combat. Byron's dad spoke at the graveside, tears streaming.

"My son was familiar with risk. He lived John 15:13, 'Greater love has no one than this: to lay down one's life for one's friends.'" He looked at Byron's mother and said, "We'll see our son again."

The sudden, twenty-one-gun salute startled me. A mournful bugle played taps. It was all too much. A two-star general took the folded American flag from the casket and presented it to Byron's mom "on behalf of a grateful nation."

That night a drawn-out reception was held at The House. Hundreds of the candles that Byron had given out over the years came back with students and alumni. Each person lit their candle as they entered The House. I did too.

Hours later I hiked up the steep hill overlooking campus with Jeb. We both took off our shoes as we walked up on the soft grass. From the top we could see the brilliant white glow of the candles in the windows lighting up The House against the darkness.

It was a House On Fire.

I wept for Byron, for Dad, and for me. All of us were home.

FOREVER IN MY HOUSE

It's been a year since the fires of Pittsburgh. I wrote a letter to my dad like he wrote one to me. He somehow knew that letter would find me. I believe someday I will deliver my letter to him in person. In the meantime, it sits near the framed letter from him in the small space they let me use in The House.

Sophie Alsas

Dad,

I got your letter from the Andes and wanted to write you back. Sorry it has taken so long.

Over the past few months I've spent time with a community of Christians who taught me about Jesus, serving others, and sacrifice. One of my friends in particular, Byron Washington, helped me understand risk in light of knowing Christ. I'm sure you've already met him. I've come to peace with the sacrifice you made for God's kingdom and I'm glad to know that as a never-ending spiritual being I will get to see you again.

I also have some news for you. I'm dating this guy Jeb. I think you'd like him. We may have an important day coming up for us soon.

I miss you Dad.

Je quiero mucho,

Sophie

I broke the arson story with Ben. We also published a multi-part story on The House. It was well-received, and Luke had to double the number of servant leadership sessions they hold for the community.

As for the arson story, Ben and I reported on the two-man arson team who were finally arrested by Dot. Both were troubled men. One had been rejected as a fireman and falsely blamed the men of Station 9 for turning him down. The arsonists were convicted of their crimes and Jeb went to visit them in federal prison. I was proud of the way he offered them forgiveness on behalf of himself and some of his fellow firemen. I went along in support. It was hard, but I hope the forgiveness helps these two to heal and choose a different path. I know it's helping Jeb and me to heal.

Jeb recovered from his injuries, but those injuries forced him to give up firefighting. He hated that, but I loved it. Instead, he went back to school for civil engineering. He still regularly hangs out at The House, only now he is a staff member working directly for Luke.

Also, Jeb has a steady girlfriend now, and it's me!

I may be the only one who knows that Jeb has "Byron Dubois Washington" and the date Byron sacrificed his life tattooed across his heart. I was there when he got the ink. We've made more than a few trips down to the mountains of southern West Virginia to see Jeb's folks. He spends a lot of time with my mom. We're getting pretty close to taking the next step in our relationship. Darcy, Mom, and Julie all approve. Max loves him too.

Byron's death was a galvanizing moment for The House, sponsoring churches, and the community. Bryon's sacrifice catalyzed a renewed commitment to discipleship. More churches got involved in sponsoring campus ministry. Ben got me connected with a faith-based online paper that I've been contributing to on the side. Currently I'm writing a series of articles on the importance of intercepting young people at a time when they're making up their minds about God.

Alumni of The House go in increasing numbers to dark places, doing good and bringing life.

As promised, Julie returned to China to establish clinics throughout her region. She spends time caring for the frail and elderly, loving everyone in her path. There is now a vibrant Christian community around her.

Darcy and I are still roommates. She decided to go back to grad school to get her Ph.D. in chemical engineering at Carnegie Mellon. She is involved with The House and loving it.

I've returned several times to Ecuador with Mom. We visited each of the churches my dad helped found. I was able to see the work he started with new eyes. It was exciting to see flourishing communities around the growing churches. I was reminded of the passage in John 12 where Jesus talks about how "when a seed dies it produces much fruit." Dad's death has produced much fruit in Ecuador, and in that I see his legacy in Christ live on.

I'm growing in my own journey. Mom and I connect every week not just as mother and daughter but to encourage each other in our walks with Christ. I'm in the Word listening to God, meditating, and memorizing scripture. I know that I am truly and forever loved.

I am starting to discern my own great purpose. I am regularly volunteering at The House and involved with alumni. There are communities taking root that focus on helping disciples lead everywhere they are living and working. I am helping to tell their stories.

Byron's sacrifice was for something. He saved lives before he got to The House. At The House he invited many students to real life with Christ. And he saved Jeb. The future cascade of this courage is big and enduring.

Byron's death helped me understand my dad. The hundred pastors he taught started a hundred churches, who have planted another hundred. Mom and I agreed to visit as many as we could.

I got a map and marked out those churches and the communities they serve. Mom and I agreed to visit every one.

I miss you, Byron. There was so much more I wanted to learn from you. I miss you, Dad. I hope you're proud of me and how far I have come. I will see you all in The House at the feast.

My dark dreams have stopped. Mom told me when I had bad dreams as a girl, dad would sing softly to me. In my new dreams I'm back in Ecuador. It's bright and the mountains are close. This time when I race toward Dad, I reach him. He is singing; singing joyfully and well. I wake up holding on to these fragments of my new dream.

POSTSCRIPT: MAKE A DIFFERENCE

So now, what do you want? What is it that you long for? I invite you to stop and think.

Early in John's Gospel, two of the disciples of John the Baptist see Jesus walk by only to hear John proclaim him to be the Lamb of God. They get excited. This must have caused a commotion. Jesus looks around, sees them, and invites them closer with a "What do you want?" He was serious. And He is serious about you. "What do you want?" The Lamb of God is asking you the same question. Those two disciples follow their desires to know and be known and ask, "Where are you staying?" They are invited: "Come, and you will see."

They choose wisely. The disciples re-orient their lives, discover the desires of their hearts, and enter an eternal kind of community. The central organizing principle of a community is being in a place where we come and see. A place where we are seen. A place where we are known and we grow to know others deeply.

Isolation is the peril of our time. We are connected digitally yet separated physically and emotionally. There is a different way.

Come and join the community of disciples and servant leaders. Fred Rogers, possibly the best known "neighbor" of all time and a beloved member of my community of Pittsburgh, reminds us "Everyone longs to be loved. And the greatest thing we can do is to let people know that they are loved and capable of loving."

If you look you will find a serving community right in your neighborhood. Come on in.

—**Rev. Lee Scott**, Coalition for Christian Outreach

JOIN THE MOVEMENT

Visit www.HouseOnFireBook.com today!

- ☐ Join the *House on Fire* Servant Leadership Community.
- ☐ Find practical resources for *Seeing Differently* and *Serving Differently.*
- ☐ Learn more about bringing Servant Leadership into your existing team, organization, or community.

ACKNOWLEDGMENTS

Ken Jennings: My life's ambition is to pursue good and great things in the company of friends, and this book is a product of that pursuit with the help of others. Heather Jennings, you made this book and our business possible. I am grateful to my co-author Mike, who leads from the pulpit and leads in life. For the writing on Afghanistan and Central Asia, I give special thanks to my son and gifted author D.L. Jennings. Dave crafted these stories. He's "been there and done that" downrange in Special Operations. Dave, you are a talented writer. I hope you write full time! I have no idea how you wrote such a terrific book, *Gift of the Shaper,* while deployed. Thanks for all you and your teammates do to keep us safe. Ashley Penman, Jessica Santacrose and Deb Lantz, thank you for your editorial work. Ashley, Jess, and Deb, you put your heart into the book and taught me how to think like a young woman. Ha! I learned a few things. Jessica Santacrose, thank you for your support on this project. I could not have made this happen without you all. John Stahl-Wert, you made me a better writer, challenging me to move beyond my current reach.

My corporate and military mentors are examples to me of doing good and great things. Thank you for your guidance and input into my life. This book reflects what I learned from all of you. To my business colleagues at Third River Partners, you all are doing great work. To my clients who have become friends, your lives and stories are a constant inspiration.

To my kids, Dave, Matt, and Sara, you are examples of leading in a way that serves others. Thank you, Jeanne Jennings, you raised good kids. And to our son Conor and wife Sarah, we are proud of all of the good you are doing together. Mom, you served us all and I love you. I hope my dad would be proud of this book. He loved and led like a servant leader and is now enjoying his upgrade.

I'll amend my first sentence in this acknowledgment. My life's ambition is to pursue Christ in the company of friends. Let's all pick up the pace and follow the leader.

Mike McCormick: *House on Fire* is truly a co-created work, and I would like to thank my co-author, Ken Jennings, for this opportunity. I appreciate Ashley Penmen, Jessica Santacrose, Niki Kapsambelis, and Heidi Cassell for your countless hours of editing. Thanks to Sara Jennings for her social media insight. Thanks to Jennifer Dorand for keeping our team on track early in the process and to Deb Lantz for willingly lending her marketing expertise. A heartfelt thanks to Heather Hyde Jennings and John Porcari for the groundwork they laid for servant ministry leaders. Thanks, also, to Morgan James for their service in the next generation of publishing.

A special thanks to Steve Crosby, Joseph Miller, Nicole Webb, and Ked Frank for their excellent Serving Leadership models that served as an inspiration for many of Sophie's interactions. I'm thankful for the Elders, staff, and congregation of Calvary Christian Church who are true ministry partners creating a greenhouse of disciple-making and leadership development. The Church is not a place it's a people, and one of my greatest privileges is to rub shoulders with these Servant Leaders.

While books are written with words, the most meaningful relationships go much deeper than words can express. With that in mind, I give my love and deepest appreciation to my wife, Kristina, for allowing my heart to feel at home with her wherever we are. I would also like to thank my children Jackson, Raegan, Jonas, and Kennedy for bringing joy into my everyday life. I am grateful for my sister, Allison, and my parents, Mike and Cathie McCormick, who have modeled lives of service and leadership for as long as I can remember. I'm also thankful for the many mentors in my life. You know the contribution you have made in my life. This work is an overflow of your investment in me.

Ultimately, I am thankful for Jesus Christ, who has entrusted to me the purpose of *equipping leaders for service*. May this book give You the honor You deserve and contribute to that eternal purpose.

ABOUT THE AUTHORS

Ken Jennings, Ph.D. - Ken Jennings is a best-selling author, speaker, and consultant in people and organizational development. Ken advises leadership teams at many healthcare, government, and non-profit organizations. He has recently worked with MCYM-Young Life, the Coalition for Christian Outreach in Pittsburgh, Johns Hopkins,  the Department of Defense, the Department of Veterans Affairs, Alignment Healthcare, Fresenius Medical Care, and other organizations.

The heart of his leadership philosophy is "putting servant leadership to work." With his business partner and wife, Heather Hyde, Ken founded Third River Partners, a Service Disabled Veteran Owned Small Business that advises organizations of all sizes in teaming, shared goal achievement, and change leadership while helping leaders to serve others.

Ken's other books include *The Serving Leader: Five Actions to Transform Your Team, Business, and Community*, co-authored with John Stahl-Wert, *The Greater Goal: Connecting Purpose and Performance*, co-authored with Health Hyde, and *Changing Health Care: Creating Tomorrow's Winning Health*

Enterprises Today, co-authored with Sharyn B. Materna and Kurt H. Miller. He holds a Ph.D. in Organizational Development from Purdue University, an M.S. in Management from the Air Force Institute of Technology, and a B.S. from the United States Air Force Academy. Ken lives in Pittsburgh and Long Island.

To learn more about Ken and Third River, please visit www.3rd-river.com

Mike McCormick, D. Min. - Mike McCormick is a people-oriented leader, trainer, and developer. He is an innovative team builder and communicator who has dedicated his life to equipping leaders to serve. Mike has been in pastoral leadership for 20 years, serving churches in Pittsburgh, Pennsylvania and Dallas,  Texas. He is currently the Lead Pastor at Calvary Christian Church (www.calvarychristian.net) in Winchester, KY, home of the soon to be famous Ale-8 soft drink. In addition to practicing Serving Leadership in his own local church and community, Mike has used his training to teach other pastors locally and internationally in the areas of preaching and leadership.

Mike also serves as a facilitator, coach, and consultant with ThirdRiver Partners in Strategy Alignment and Serving Leader Development. He has served organizations such as: Military Community Youth Ministries, Refuge for Women, Genesis Healthcare, Johns Hopkins Medicine, West Virginia University Medicine, and Sisters of Charity Health System.

Mike is a frequent speaker on putting Serving Leadership to work and has been a presenter at the *Robert Greenleaf Center for Servant Leadership Conference.*

Mike received his Th.M. and D.Min from Dallas Theological Seminary, with a focus on *Leadership Development in Fast Growing Multi-site Churches*. He received a B.A. in Communications from Asbury University. Mike loves Star Wars, Pittsburgh Steelers football, and University of Kentucky Basketball. He lives in Kentucky with his wife, Kristina, and their four children Jackson, Raegan, Jonas, and Kennedy.

Lightning Source UK Ltd.
Milton Keynes UK
UKHW041146100820
367991UK00001B/101

9 781642 794878